C-736   CAREER EXAMINATION SERIES

This is your
PASSBOOK for...

Sheet Metal Worker

Test Preparation Study Guide
Questions & Answers

NLC®

NATIONAL LEARNING CORPORATION®

COPYRIGHT NOTICE

This book is SOLELY intended for, is sold ONLY to, and its use is RESTRICTED to individual, bona fide applicants or candidates who qualify by virtue of having seriously filed applications for appropriate license, certificate, professional and/or promotional advancement, higher school matriculation, scholarship, or other legitimate requirements of education and/or governmental authorities.

This book is NOT intended for use, class instruction, tutoring, training, duplication, copying, reprinting, excerption, or adaptation, etc., by:

1) Other publishers
2) Proprietors and/or Instructors of "Coaching" and/or Preparatory Courses
3) Personnel and/or Training Divisions of commercial, industrial, and governmental organizations
4) Schools, colleges, or universities and/or their departments and staffs, including teachers and other personnel
5) Testing Agencies or Bureaus
6) Study groups which seek by the purchase of a single volume to copy and/or duplicate and/or adapt this material for use by the group as a whole without having purchased individual volumes for each of the members of the group
7) Et al.

Such persons would be in violation of appropriate Federal and State statutes.

PROVISION OF LICENSING AGREEMENTS – Recognized educational, commercial, industrial, and governmental institutions and organizations, and others legitimately engaged in educational pursuits, including training, testing, and measurement activities, may address request for a licensing agreement to the copyright owners, who will determine whether, and under what conditions, including fees and charges, the materials in this book may be used them. In other words, a licensing facility exists for the legitimate use of the material in this book on other than an individual basis. However, it is asseverated and affirmed here that the material in this book CANNOT be used without the receipt of the express permission of such a licensing agreement from the Publishers. Inquiries re licensing should be addressed to the company, attention rights and permissions department.

All rights reserved, including the right of reproduction in whole or in part, in any form or by any means, electronic or mechanical, including photocopying, recording, or by any information storage and retrieval system, without permission in writing from the Publisher.

Copyright © 2024 by
National Learning Corporation

212 Michael Drive, Syosset, NY 11791
(516) 921-8888 • www.passbooks.com
E-mail: info@passbooks.com

PUBLISHED IN THE UNITED STATES OF AMERICA

PASSBOOK® SERIES

THE *PASSBOOK® SERIES* has been created to prepare applicants and candidates for the ultimate academic battlefield – the examination room.

At some time in our lives, each and every one of us may be required to take an examination – for validation, matriculation, admission, qualification, registration, certification, or licensure.

Based on the assumption that every applicant or candidate has met the basic formal educational standards, has taken the required number of courses, and read the necessary texts, the *PASSBOOK® SERIES* furnishes the one special preparation which may assure passing with confidence, instead of failing with insecurity. Examination questions – together with answers – are furnished as the basic vehicle for study so that the mysteries of the examination and its compounding difficulties may be eliminated or diminished by a sure method.

This book is meant to help you pass your examination provided that you qualify and are serious in your objective.

The entire field is reviewed through the huge store of content information which is succinctly presented through a provocative and challenging approach – the question-and-answer method.

A climate of success is established by furnishing the correct answers at the end of each test.

You soon learn to recognize types of questions, forms of questions, and patterns of questioning. You may even begin to anticipate expected outcomes.

You perceive that many questions are repeated or adapted so that you can gain acute insights, which may enable you to score many sure points.

You learn how to confront new questions, or types of questions, and to attack them confidently and work out the correct answers.

You note objectives and emphases, and recognize pitfalls and dangers, so that you may make positive educational adjustments.

Moreover, you are kept fully informed in relation to new concepts, methods, practices, and directions in the field.

You discover that you are actually taking the examination all the time: you are preparing for the examination by "taking" an examination, not by reading extraneous and/or supererogatory textbooks.

In short, this PASSBOOK®, used directedly, should be an important factor in helping you to pass your test.

SHEET METAL WORKER

JOB DESCRIPTION

Under supervision, fabricates, erects, and repairs sheet metal structures such as ducts, metal ceilings, tanks, storm louvres, roofs, etc.; performs related work.

EXAMPLES OF TYPICAL TASKS

Lays out, cuts, shapes, forms, rivets, spot welds, solders and sweats tin, copper, brass and all forms of sheet metal. Sets and erects sheet metal structures such as ducts, louvres, canvas connections, ceilings, dampers, etc. Develops patterns and templates in fabricating complex shapes and forms. Repairs metal ceilings, roofs, leaders, gutters, etc. Does simple rigging in making these repairs. Supervises assigned personnel. Keeps work records.

TEST

The written test will be of the multiple-choice type and may include questions on sheet metal fabrication, erection, repair and shop practices; materials, tools, equipment and rigging; pattern and template making, related mathematics and reading comprehension, reports, safety and other related areas.

HOW TO TAKE A TEST

I. YOU MUST PASS AN EXAMINATION

A. WHAT EVERY CANDIDATE SHOULD KNOW

Examination applicants often ask us for help in preparing for the written test. What can I study in advance? What kinds of questions will be asked? How will the test be given? How will the papers be graded?

As an applicant for a civil service examination, you may be wondering about some of these things. Our purpose here is to suggest effective methods of advance study and to describe civil service examinations.

Your chances for success on this examination can be increased if you know how to prepare. Those "pre-examination jitters" can be reduced if you know what to expect. You can even experience an adventure in good citizenship if you know why civil service exams are given.

B. WHY ARE CIVIL SERVICE EXAMINATIONS GIVEN?

Civil service examinations are important to you in two ways. As a citizen, you want public jobs filled by employees who know how to do their work. As a job seeker, you want a fair chance to compete for that job on an equal footing with other candidates. The best-known means of accomplishing this two-fold goal is the competitive examination.

Exams are widely publicized throughout the nation. They may be administered for jobs in federal, state, city, municipal, town or village governments or agencies.

Any citizen may apply, with some limitations, such as the age or residence of applicants. Your experience and education may be reviewed to see whether you meet the requirements for the particular examination. When these requirements exist, they are reasonable and applied consistently to all applicants. Thus, a competitive examination may cause you some uneasiness now, but it is your privilege and safeguard.

C. HOW ARE CIVIL SERVICE EXAMS DEVELOPED?

Examinations are carefully written by trained technicians who are specialists in the field known as "psychological measurement," in consultation with recognized authorities in the field of work that the test will cover. These experts recommend the subject matter areas or skills to be tested; only those knowledges or skills important to your success on the job are included. The most reliable books and source materials available are used as references. Together, the experts and technicians judge the difficulty level of the questions.

Test technicians know how to phrase questions so that the problem is clearly stated. Their ethics do not permit "trick" or "catch" questions. Questions may have been tried out on sample groups, or subjected to statistical analysis, to determine their usefulness.

Written tests are often used in combination with performance tests, ratings of training and experience, and oral interviews. All of these measures combine to form the best-known means of finding the right person for the right job.

II. HOW TO PASS THE WRITTEN TEST

A. NATURE OF THE EXAMINATION

To prepare intelligently for civil service examinations, you should know how they differ from school examinations you have taken. In school you were assigned certain definite pages to read or subjects to cover. The examination questions were quite detailed and usually emphasized memory. Civil service exams, on the other hand, try to discover your present ability to perform the duties of a position, plus your potentiality to learn these duties. In other words, a civil service exam attempts to predict how successful you will be. Questions cover such a broad area that they cannot be as minute and detailed as school exam questions.

In the public service similar kinds of work, or positions, are grouped together in one "class." This process is known as *position-classification*. All the positions in a class are paid according to the salary range for that class. One class title covers all of these positions, and they are all tested by the same examination.

B. FOUR BASIC STEPS

1) Study the announcement

How, then, can you know what subjects to study? Our best answer is: "Learn as much as possible about the class of positions for which you've applied." The exam will test the knowledge, skills and abilities needed to do the work.

Your most valuable source of information about the position you want is the official exam announcement. This announcement lists the training and experience qualifications. Check these standards and apply only if you come reasonably close to meeting them.

The brief description of the position in the examination announcement offers some clues to the subjects which will be tested. Think about the job itself. Review the duties in your mind. Can you perform them, or are there some in which you are rusty? Fill in the blank spots in your preparation.

Many jurisdictions preview the written test in the exam announcement by including a section called "Knowledge and Abilities Required," "Scope of the Examination," or some similar heading. Here you will find out specifically what fields will be tested.

2) Review your own background

Once you learn in general what the position is all about, and what you need to know to do the work, ask yourself which subjects you already know fairly well and which need improvement. You may wonder whether to concentrate on improving your strong areas or on building some background in your fields of weakness. When the announcement has specified "some knowledge" or "considerable knowledge," or has used adjectives like "beginning principles of..." or "advanced ... methods," you can get a clue as to the number and difficulty of questions to be asked in any given field. More questions, and hence broader coverage, would be included for those subjects which are more important in the work. Now weigh your strengths and weaknesses against the job requirements and prepare accordingly.

3) Determine the level of the position

Another way to tell how intensively you should prepare is to understand the level of the job for which you are applying. Is it the entering level? In other words, is this the position in which beginners in a field of work are hired? Or is it an intermediate or advanced level? Sometimes this is indicated by such words as "Junior" or "Senior" in the class title. Other jurisdictions use Roman numerals to designate the level – Clerk I, Clerk II, for example. The word "Supervisor" sometimes appears in the title. If the level is not indicated by the title, check the description of duties. Will you be working under very close supervision, or will you have responsibility for independent decisions in this work?

4) Choose appropriate study materials

Now that you know the subjects to be examined and the relative amount of each subject to be covered, you can choose suitable study materials. For beginning level jobs, or even advanced ones, if you have a pronounced weakness in some aspect of your training, read a modern, standard textbook in that field. Be sure it is up to date and has general coverage. Such books are normally available at your library, and the librarian will be glad to help you locate one. For entry-level positions, questions of appropriate difficulty are chosen — neither highly advanced questions, nor those too simple. Such questions require careful thought but not advanced training.

If the position for which you are applying is technical or advanced, you will read more advanced, specialized material. If you are already familiar with the basic principles of your field, elementary textbooks would waste your time. Concentrate on advanced textbooks and technical periodicals. Think through the concepts and review difficult problems in your field.

These are all general sources. You can get more ideas on your own initiative, following these leads. For example, training manuals and publications of the government agency which employs workers in your field can be useful, particularly for technical and professional positions. A letter or visit to the government department involved may result in more specific study suggestions, and certainly will provide you with a more definite idea of the exact nature of the position you are seeking.

III. KINDS OF TESTS

Tests are used for purposes other than measuring knowledge and ability to perform specified duties. For some positions, it is equally important to test ability to make adjustments to new situations or to profit from training. In others, basic mental abilities not dependent on information are essential. Questions which test these things may not appear as pertinent to the duties of the position as those which test for knowledge and information. Yet they are often highly important parts of a fair examination. For very general questions, it is almost impossible to help you direct your study efforts. What we can do is to point out some of the more common of these general abilities needed in public service positions and describe some typical questions.

1) General information

Broad, general information has been found useful for predicting job success in some kinds of work. This is tested in a variety of ways, from vocabulary lists to questions about current events. Basic background in some field of work, such as sociology or economics, may be sampled in a group of questions. Often these are principles which have become familiar to most persons through exposure rather than through formal training. It is difficult to advise you how to study for these questions; being alert to the world around you is our best suggestion.

2) Verbal ability

An example of an ability needed in many positions is verbal or language ability. Verbal ability is, in brief, the ability to use and understand words. Vocabulary and grammar tests are typical measures of this ability. Reading comprehension or paragraph interpretation questions are common in many kinds of civil service tests. You are given a paragraph of written material and asked to find its central meaning.

3) Numerical ability

Number skills can be tested by the familiar arithmetic problem, by checking paired lists of numbers to see which are alike and which are different, or by interpreting charts and graphs. In the latter test, a graph may be printed in the test booklet which you are asked to use as the basis for answering questions.

4) Observation

A popular test for law-enforcement positions is the observation test. A picture is shown to you for several minutes, then taken away. Questions about the picture test your ability to observe both details and larger elements.

5) Following directions

In many positions in the public service, the employee must be able to carry out written instructions dependably and accurately. You may be given a chart with several columns, each column listing a variety of information. The questions require you to carry out directions involving the information given in the chart.

6) Skills and aptitudes

Performance tests effectively measure some manual skills and aptitudes. When the skill is one in which you are trained, such as typing or shorthand, you can practice. These tests are often very much like those given in business school or high school courses. For many of the other skills and aptitudes, however, no short-time preparation can be made. Skills and abilities natural to you or that you have developed throughout your lifetime are being tested.

Many of the general questions just described provide all the data needed to answer the questions and ask you to use your reasoning ability to find the answers. Your best preparation for these tests, as well as for tests of facts and ideas, is to be at your physical and mental best. You, no doubt, have your own methods of getting into an exam-taking mood and keeping "in shape." The next section lists some ideas on this subject.

IV. KINDS OF QUESTIONS

Only rarely is the "essay" question, which you answer in narrative form, used in civil service tests. Civil service tests are usually of the short-answer type. Full instructions for answering these questions will be given to you at the examination. But in case this is your first experience with short-answer questions and separate answer sheets, here is what you need to know:

1) Multiple-choice Questions

Most popular of the short-answer questions is the "multiple choice" or "best answer" question. It can be used, for example, to test for factual knowledge, ability to solve problems or judgment in meeting situations found at work.

A multiple-choice question is normally one of three types—
- It can begin with an incomplete statement followed by several possible endings. You are to find the one ending which *best* completes the statement, although some of the others may not be entirely wrong.
- It can also be a complete statement in the form of a question which is answered by choosing one of the statements listed.

- It can be in the form of a problem – again you select the best answer.

Here is an example of a multiple-choice question with a discussion which should give you some clues as to the method for choosing the right answer:

When an employee has a complaint about his assignment, the action which will *best* help him overcome his difficulty is to
- A. discuss his difficulty with his coworkers
- B. take the problem to the head of the organization
- C. take the problem to the person who gave him the assignment
- D. say nothing to anyone about his complaint

In answering this question, you should study each of the choices to find which is best. Consider choice "A" – Certainly an employee may discuss his complaint with fellow employees, but no change or improvement can result, and the complaint remains unresolved. Choice "B" is a poor choice since the head of the organization probably does not know what assignment you have been given, and taking your problem to him is known as "going over the head" of the supervisor. The supervisor, or person who made the assignment, is the person who can clarify it or correct any injustice. Choice "C" is, therefore, correct. To say nothing, as in choice "D," is unwise. Supervisors have and interest in knowing the problems employees are facing, and the employee is seeking a solution to his problem.

2) True/False Questions

The "true/false" or "right/wrong" form of question is sometimes used. Here a complete statement is given. Your job is to decide whether the statement is right or wrong.

SAMPLE: A roaming cell-phone call to a nearby city costs less than a non-roaming call to a distant city.

This statement is wrong, or false, since roaming calls are more expensive.

This is not a complete list of all possible question forms, although most of the others are variations of these common types. You will always get complete directions for answering questions. Be sure you understand *how* to mark your answers – ask questions until you do.

V. RECORDING YOUR ANSWERS

Computer terminals are used more and more today for many different kinds of exams.

For an examination with very few applicants, you may be told to record your answers in the test booklet itself. Separate answer sheets are much more common. If this separate answer sheet is to be scored by machine – and this is often the case – it is highly important that you mark your answers correctly in order to get credit.

An electronic scoring machine is often used in civil service offices because of the speed with which papers can be scored. Machine-scored answer sheets must be marked with a pencil, which will be given to you. This pencil has a high graphite content which responds to the electronic scoring machine. As a matter of fact, stray dots may register as answers, so do not let your pencil rest on the answer sheet while you are pondering the correct answer. Also, if your pencil lead breaks or is otherwise defective, ask for another.

Since the answer sheet will be dropped in a slot in the scoring machine, be careful not to bend the corners or get the paper crumpled.

The answer sheet normally has five vertical columns of numbers, with 30 numbers to a column. These numbers correspond to the question numbers in your test booklet. After each number, going across the page are four or five pairs of dotted lines. These short dotted lines have small letters or numbers above them. The first two pairs may also have a "T" or "F" above the letters. This indicates that the first two pairs only are to be used if the questions are of the true-false type. If the questions are multiple choice, disregard the "T" and "F" and pay attention only to the small letters or numbers.

Answer your questions in the manner of the sample that follows:

32. The largest city in the United States is
    A. Washington, D.C.
    B. New York City
    C. Chicago
    D. Detroit
    E. San Francisco

1) Choose the answer you think is best. (New York City is the largest, so "B" is correct.)
2) Find the row of dotted lines numbered the same as the question you are answering. (Find row number 32)
3) Find the pair of dotted lines corresponding to the answer. (Find the pair of lines under the mark "B.")
4) Make a solid black mark between the dotted lines.

VI. BEFORE THE TEST

Common sense will help you find procedures to follow to get ready for an examination. Too many of us, however, overlook these sensible measures. Indeed, nervousness and fatigue have been found to be the most serious reasons why applicants fail to do their best on civil service tests. Here is a list of reminders:

- Begin your preparation early – Don't wait until the last minute to go scurrying around for books and materials or to find out what the position is all about.
- Prepare continuously – An hour a night for a week is better than an all-night cram session. This has been definitely established. What is more, a night a week for a month will return better dividends than crowding your study into a shorter period of time.
- Locate the place of the exam – You have been sent a notice telling you when and where to report for the examination. If the location is in a different town or otherwise unfamiliar to you, it would be well to inquire the best route and learn something about the building.
- Relax the night before the test – Allow your mind to rest. Do not study at all that night. Plan some mild recreation or diversion; then go to bed early and get a good night's sleep.
- Get up early enough to make a leisurely trip to the place for the test – This way unforeseen events, traffic snarls, unfamiliar buildings, etc. will not upset you.
- Dress comfortably – A written test is not a fashion show. You will be known by number and not by name, so wear something comfortable.

- Leave excess paraphernalia at home – Shopping bags and odd bundles will get in your way. You need bring only the items mentioned in the official notice you received; usually everything you need is provided. Do not bring reference books to the exam. They will only confuse those last minutes and be taken away from you when in the test room.
- Arrive somewhat ahead of time – If because of transportation schedules you must get there very early, bring a newspaper or magazine to take your mind off yourself while waiting.
- Locate the examination room – When you have found the proper room, you will be directed to the seat or part of the room where you will sit. Sometimes you are given a sheet of instructions to read while you are waiting. Do not fill out any forms until you are told to do so; just read them and be prepared.
- Relax and prepare to listen to the instructions
- If you have any physical problem that may keep you from doing your best, be sure to tell the test administrator. If you are sick or in poor health, you really cannot do your best on the exam. You can come back and take the test some other time.

VII. AT THE TEST

The day of the test is here and you have the test booklet in your hand. The temptation to get going is very strong. Caution! There is more to success than knowing the right answers. You must know how to identify your papers and understand variations in the type of short-answer question used in this particular examination. Follow these suggestions for maximum results from your efforts:

1) Cooperate with the monitor

The test administrator has a duty to create a situation in which you can be as much at ease as possible. He will give instructions, tell you when to begin, check to see that you are marking your answer sheet correctly, and so on. He is not there to guard you, although he will see that your competitors do not take unfair advantage. He wants to help you do your best.

2) Listen to all instructions

Don't jump the gun! Wait until you understand all directions. In most civil service tests you get more time than you need to answer the questions. So don't be in a hurry. Read each word of instructions until you clearly understand the meaning. Study the examples, listen to all announcements and follow directions. Ask questions if you do not understand what to do.

3) Identify your papers

Civil service exams are usually identified by number only. You will be assigned a number; you must not put your name on your test papers. Be sure to copy your number correctly. Since more than one exam may be given, copy your exact examination title.

4) Plan your time

Unless you are told that a test is a "speed" or "rate of work" test, speed itself is usually not important. Time enough to answer all the questions will be provided, but this does not mean that you have all day. An overall time limit has been set. Divide the total time (in minutes) by the number of questions to determine the approximate time you have for each question.

5) Do not linger over difficult questions

If you come across a difficult question, mark it with a paper clip (useful to have along) and come back to it when you have been through the booklet. One caution if you do this – be sure to skip a number on your answer sheet as well. Check often to be sure that you have not lost your place and that you are marking in the row numbered the same as the question you are answering.

6) Read the questions

Be sure you know what the question asks! Many capable people are unsuccessful because they failed to *read* the questions correctly.

7) Answer all questions

Unless you have been instructed that a penalty will be deducted for incorrect answers, it is better to guess than to omit a question.

8) Speed tests

It is often better NOT to guess on speed tests. It has been found that on timed tests people are tempted to spend the last few seconds before time is called in marking answers at random – without even reading them – in the hope of picking up a few extra points. To discourage this practice, the instructions may warn you that your score will be "corrected" for guessing. That is, a penalty will be applied. The incorrect answers will be deducted from the correct ones, or some other penalty formula will be used.

9) Review your answers

If you finish before time is called, go back to the questions you guessed or omitted to give them further thought. Review other answers if you have time.

10) Return your test materials

If you are ready to leave before others have finished or time is called, take ALL your materials to the monitor and leave quietly. Never take any test material with you. The monitor can discover whose papers are not complete, and taking a test booklet may be grounds for disqualification.

VIII. EXAMINATION TECHNIQUES

1) Read the general instructions carefully. These are usually printed on the first page of the exam booklet. As a rule, these instructions refer to the timing of the examination; the fact that you should not start work until the signal and must stop work at a signal, etc. If there are any *special* instructions, such as a choice of questions to be answered, make sure that you note this instruction carefully.

2) When you are ready to start work on the examination, that is as soon as the signal has been given, read the instructions to each question booklet, underline any key words or phrases, such as *least, best, outline, describe* and the like. In this way you will tend to answer as requested rather than discover on reviewing your paper that you *listed without describing*, that you selected the *worst* choice rather than the *best* choice, etc.

3) If the examination is of the objective or multiple-choice type – that is, each question will also give a series of possible answers: A, B, C or D, and you are called upon to select the best answer and write the letter next to that answer on your answer paper – it is advisable to start answering each question in turn. There may be anywhere from 50 to 100 such questions in the three or four hours allotted and you can see how much time would be taken if you read through all the questions before beginning to answer any. Furthermore, if you come across a question or group of questions which you know would be difficult to answer, it would undoubtedly affect your handling of all the other questions.

4) If the examination is of the essay type and contains but a few questions, it is a moot point as to whether you should read all the questions before starting to answer any one. Of course, if you are given a choice – say five out of seven and the like – then it is essential to read all the questions so you can eliminate the two that are most difficult. If, however, you are asked to answer all the questions, there may be danger in trying to answer the easiest one first because you may find that you will spend too much time on it. The best technique is to answer the first question, then proceed to the second, etc.

5) Time your answers. Before the exam begins, write down the time it started, then add the time allowed for the examination and write down the time it must be completed, then divide the time available somewhat as follows:
    - If 3-1/2 hours are allowed, that would be 210 minutes. If you have 80 objective-type questions, that would be an average of 2-1/2 minutes per question. Allow yourself no more than 2 minutes per question, or a total of 160 minutes, which will permit about 50 minutes to review.
    - If for the time allotment of 210 minutes there are 7 essay questions to answer, that would average about 30 minutes a question. Give yourself only 25 minutes per question so that you have about 35 minutes to review.

6) The most important instruction is to *read each question* and make sure you know what is wanted. The second most important instruction is to *time yourself properly* so that you answer every question. The third most important instruction is to *answer every question*. Guess if you have to but include something for each question. Remember that you will receive no credit for a blank and will probably receive some credit if you write something in answer to an essay question. If you guess a letter – say "B" for a multiple-choice question – you may have guessed right. If you leave a blank as an answer to a multiple-choice question, the examiners may respect your feelings but it will not add a point to your score. Some exams may penalize you for wrong answers, so in such cases *only*, you may not want to guess unless you have some basis for your answer.

7) Suggestions
    a. Objective-type questions
        1. Examine the question booklet for proper sequence of pages and questions
        2. Read all instructions carefully
        3. Skip any question which seems too difficult; return to it after all other questions have been answered
        4. Apportion your time properly; do not spend too much time on any single question or group of questions

5. Note and underline key words – *all, most, fewest, least, best, worst, same, opposite,* etc.
6. Pay particular attention to negatives
7. Note unusual option, e.g., unduly long, short, complex, different or similar in content to the body of the question
8. Observe the use of "hedging" words – *probably, may, most likely,* etc.
9. Make sure that your answer is put next to the same number as the question
10. Do not second-guess unless you have good reason to believe the second answer is definitely more correct
11. Cross out original answer if you decide another answer is more accurate; do not erase until you are ready to hand your paper in
12. Answer all questions; guess unless instructed otherwise
13. Leave time for review

   b. Essay questions
1. Read each question carefully
2. Determine exactly what is wanted. Underline key words or phrases.
3. Decide on outline or paragraph answer
4. Include many different points and elements unless asked to develop any one or two points or elements
5. Show impartiality by giving pros and cons unless directed to select one side only
6. Make and write down any assumptions you find necessary to answer the questions
7. Watch your English, grammar, punctuation and choice of words
8. Time your answers; don't crowd material

8) Answering the essay question

Most essay questions can be answered by framing the specific response around several key words or ideas. Here are a few such key words or ideas:

M's: manpower, materials, methods, money, management
P's: purpose, program, policy, plan, procedure, practice, problems, pitfalls, personnel, public relations

   a. Six basic steps in handling problems:
1. Preliminary plan and background development
2. Collect information, data and facts
3. Analyze and interpret information, data and facts
4. Analyze and develop solutions as well as make recommendations
5. Prepare report and sell recommendations
6. Install recommendations and follow up effectiveness

   b. Pitfalls to avoid
1. *Taking things for granted* – A statement of the situation does not necessarily imply that each of the elements is necessarily true; for example, a complaint may be invalid and biased so that all that can be taken for granted is that a complaint has been registered

2. *Considering only one side of a situation* – Wherever possible, indicate several alternatives and then point out the reasons you selected the best one
3. *Failing to indicate follow up* – Whenever your answer indicates action on your part, make certain that you will take proper follow-up action to see how successful your recommendations, procedures or actions turn out to be
4. *Taking too long in answering any single question* – Remember to time your answers properly

IX. AFTER THE TEST

Scoring procedures differ in detail among civil service jurisdictions although the general principles are the same. Whether the papers are hand-scored or graded by machine we have described, they are nearly always graded by number. That is, the person who marks the paper knows only the number – never the name – of the applicant. Not until all the papers have been graded will they be matched with names. If other tests, such as training and experience or oral interview ratings have been given, scores will be combined. Different parts of the examination usually have different weights. For example, the written test might count 60 percent of the final grade, and a rating of training and experience 40 percent. In many jurisdictions, veterans will have a certain number of points added to their grades.

After the final grade has been determined, the names are placed in grade order and an eligible list is established. There are various methods for resolving ties between those who get the same final grade – probably the most common is to place first the name of the person whose application was received first. Job offers are made from the eligible list in the order the names appear on it. You will be notified of your grade and your rank as soon as all these computations have been made. This will be done as rapidly as possible.

People who are found to meet the requirements in the announcement are called "eligibles." Their names are put on a list of eligible candidates. An eligible's chances of getting a job depend on how high he stands on this list and how fast agencies are filling jobs from the list.

When a job is to be filled from a list of eligibles, the agency asks for the names of people on the list of eligibles for that job. When the civil service commission receives this request, it sends to the agency the names of the three people highest on this list. Or, if the job to be filled has specialized requirements, the office sends the agency the names of the top three persons who meet these requirements from the general list.

The appointing officer makes a choice from among the three people whose names were sent to him. If the selected person accepts the appointment, the names of the others are put back on the list to be considered for future openings.

That is the rule in hiring from all kinds of eligible lists, whether they are for typist, carpenter, chemist, or something else. For every vacancy, the appointing officer has his choice of any one of the top three eligibles on the list. This explains why the person whose name is on top of the list sometimes does not get an appointment when some of the persons lower on the list do. If the appointing officer chooses the second or third eligible, the No. 1 eligible does not get a job at once, but stays on the list until he is appointed or the list is terminated.

X. HOW TO PASS THE INTERVIEW TEST

The examination for which you applied requires an oral interview test. You have already taken the written test and you are now being called for the interview test – the final part of the formal examination.

You may think that it is not possible to prepare for an interview test and that there are no procedures to follow during an interview. Our purpose is to point out some things you can do in advance that will help you and some good rules to follow and pitfalls to avoid while you are being interviewed.

What is an interview supposed to test?

The written examination is designed to test the technical knowledge and competence of the candidate; the oral is designed to evaluate intangible qualities, not readily measured otherwise, and to establish a list showing the relative fitness of each candidate – as measured against his competitors – for the position sought. Scoring is not on the basis of "right" and "wrong," but on a sliding scale of values ranging from "not passable" to "outstanding." As a matter of fact, it is possible to achieve a relatively low score without a single "incorrect" answer because of evident weakness in the qualities being measured.

Occasionally, an examination may consist entirely of an oral test – either an individual or a group oral. In such cases, information is sought concerning the technical knowledges and abilities of the candidate, since there has been no written examination for this purpose. More commonly, however, an oral test is used to supplement a written examination.

Who conducts interviews?

The composition of oral boards varies among different jurisdictions. In nearly all, a representative of the personnel department serves as chairman. One of the members of the board may be a representative of the department in which the candidate would work. In some cases, "outside experts" are used, and, frequently, a businessman or some other representative of the general public is asked to serve. Labor and management or other special groups may be represented. The aim is to secure the services of experts in the appropriate field.

However the board is composed, it is a good idea (and not at all improper or unethical) to ascertain in advance of the interview who the members are and what groups they represent. When you are introduced to them, you will have some idea of their backgrounds and interests, and at least you will not stutter and stammer over their names.

What should be done before the interview?

While knowledge about the board members is useful and takes some of the surprise element out of the interview, there is other preparation which is more substantive. It *is* possible to prepare for an oral interview – in several ways:

1) Keep a copy of your application and review it carefully before the interview

This may be the only document before the oral board, and the starting point of the interview. Know what education and experience you have listed there, and the sequence and dates of all of it. Sometimes the board will ask you to review the highlights of your experience for them; you should not have to hem and haw doing it.

2) Study the class specification and the examination announcement

Usually, the oral board has one or both of these to guide them. The qualities, characteristics or knowledges required by the position sought are stated in these documents. They offer valuable clues as to the nature of the oral interview. For example, if the job involves supervisory responsibilities, the announcement will usually indicate that knowledge of modern supervisory methods and the qualifications of the candidate as a supervisor will be tested. If so, you can expect such questions, frequently in the form of a hypothetical situation which you are expected to solve. NEVER go into an oral without knowledge of the duties and responsibilities of the job you seek.

3) Think through each qualification required

Try to visualize the kind of questions you would ask if you were a board member. How well could you answer them? Try especially to appraise your own knowledge and background in each area, *measured against the job sought*, and identify any areas in which you are weak. Be critical and realistic – do not flatter yourself.

4) Do some general reading in areas in which you feel you may be weak

For example, if the job involves supervision and your past experience has NOT, some general reading in supervisory methods and practices, particularly in the field of human relations, might be useful. Do NOT study agency procedures or detailed manuals. The oral board will be testing your understanding and capacity, not your memory.

5) Get a good night's sleep and watch your general health and mental attitude

You will want a clear head at the interview. Take care of a cold or any other minor ailment, and of course, no hangovers.

What should be done on the day of the interview?

Now comes the day of the interview itself. Give yourself plenty of time to get there. Plan to arrive somewhat ahead of the scheduled time, particularly if your appointment is in the fore part of the day. If a previous candidate fails to appear, the board might be ready for you a bit early. By early afternoon an oral board is almost invariably behind schedule if there are many candidates, and you may have to wait. Take along a book or magazine to read, or your application to review, but leave any extraneous material in the waiting room when you go in for your interview. In any event, relax and compose yourself.

The matter of dress is important. The board is forming impressions about you – from your experience, your manners, your attitude, and your appearance. Give your personal appearance careful attention. Dress your best, but not your flashiest. Choose conservative, appropriate clothing, and be sure it is immaculate. This is a business interview, and your appearance should indicate that you regard it as such. Besides, being well groomed and properly dressed will help boost your confidence.

Sooner or later, someone will call your name and escort you into the interview room. *This is it.* From here on you are on your own. It is too late for any more preparation. But remember, you asked for this opportunity to prove your fitness, and you are here because your request was granted.

What happens when you go in?

The usual sequence of events will be as follows: The clerk (who is often the board stenographer) will introduce you to the chairman of the oral board, who will introduce you to the other members of the board. Acknowledge the introductions before you sit down. Do not be surprised if you find a microphone facing you or a stenotypist sitting by. Oral interviews are usually recorded in the event of an appeal or other review.

Usually the chairman of the board will open the interview by reviewing the highlights of your education and work experience from your application – primarily for the benefit of the other members of the board, as well as to get the material into the record. Do not interrupt or comment unless there is an error or significant misinterpretation; if that is the case, do not hesitate. But do not quibble about insignificant matters. Also, he will usually ask you some question about your education, experience or your present job – partly to get you to start talking and to establish the interviewing "rapport." He may start the actual questioning, or turn it over to one of the other members. Frequently, each member undertakes the questioning on a particular area, one in which he is perhaps most competent, so you can expect each member to participate in the examination. Because time is limited, you may also expect some rather abrupt switches in the direction the questioning takes, so do not be upset by it. Normally, a board member will not pursue a single line of questioning unless he discovers a particular strength or weakness.

After each member has participated, the chairman will usually ask whether any member has any further questions, then will ask you if you have anything you wish to add. Unless you are expecting this question, it may floor you. Worse, it may start you off on an extended, extemporaneous speech. The board is not usually seeking more information. The question is principally to offer you a last opportunity to present further qualifications or to indicate that you have nothing to add. So, if you feel that a significant qualification or characteristic has been overlooked, it is proper to point it out in a sentence or so. Do not compliment the board on the thoroughness of their examination – they have been sketchy, and you know it. If you wish, merely say, "No thank you, I have nothing further to add." This is a point where you can "talk yourself out" of a good impression or fail to present an important bit of information. Remember, *you close the interview yourself.*

The chairman will then say, "That is all, Mr. _____, thank you." Do not be startled; the interview is over, and quicker than you think. Thank him, gather your belongings and take your leave. Save your sigh of relief for the other side of the door.

How to put your best foot forward
Throughout this entire process, you may feel that the board individually and collectively is trying to pierce your defenses, seek out your hidden weaknesses and embarrass and confuse you. Actually, this is not true. They are obliged to make an appraisal of your qualifications for the job you are seeking, and they want to see you in your best light. Remember, they must interview all candidates and a non-cooperative candidate may become a failure in spite of their best efforts to bring out his qualifications. Here are 15 suggestions that will help you:

1) Be natural – Keep your attitude confident, not cocky
If you are not confident that you can do the job, do not expect the board to be. Do not apologize for your weaknesses, try to bring out your strong points. The board is interested in a positive, not negative, presentation. Cockiness will antagonize any board member and make him wonder if you are covering up a weakness by a false show of strength.

2) Get comfortable, but don't lounge or sprawl
Sit erectly but not stiffly. A careless posture may lead the board to conclude that you are careless in other things, or at least that you are not impressed by the importance of the occasion. Either conclusion is natural, even if incorrect. Do not fuss with your clothing, a pencil or an ashtray. Your hands may occasionally be useful to emphasize a point; do not let them become a point of distraction.

3) Do not wisecrack or make small talk
This is a serious situation, and your attitude should show that you consider it as such. Further, the time of the board is limited – they do not want to waste it, and neither should you.

4) Do not exaggerate your experience or abilities

In the first place, from information in the application or other interviews and sources, the board may know more about you than you think. Secondly, you probably will not get away with it. An experienced board is rather adept at spotting such a situation, so do not take the chance.

5) If you know a board member, do not make a point of it, yet do not hide it

Certainly you are not fooling him, and probably not the other members of the board. Do not try to take advantage of your acquaintanceship – it will probably do you little good.

6) Do not dominate the interview

Let the board do that. They will give you the clues – do not assume that you have to do all the talking. Realize that the board has a number of questions to ask you, and do not try to take up all the interview time by showing off your extensive knowledge of the answer to the first one.

7) Be attentive

You only have 20 minutes or so, and you should keep your attention at its sharpest throughout. When a member is addressing a problem or question to you, give him your undivided attention. Address your reply principally to him, but do not exclude the other board members.

8) Do not interrupt

A board member may be stating a problem for you to analyze. He will ask you a question when the time comes. Let him state the problem, and wait for the question.

9) Make sure you understand the question

Do not try to answer until you are sure what the question is. If it is not clear, restate it in your own words or ask the board member to clarify it for you. However, do not haggle about minor elements.

10) Reply promptly but not hastily

A common entry on oral board rating sheets is "candidate responded readily," or "candidate hesitated in replies." Respond as promptly and quickly as you can, but do not jump to a hasty, ill-considered answer.

11) Do not be peremptory in your answers

A brief answer is proper – but do not fire your answer back. That is a losing game from your point of view. The board member can probably ask questions much faster than you can answer them.

12) Do not try to create the answer you think the board member wants

He is interested in what kind of mind you have and how it works – not in playing games. Furthermore, he can usually spot this practice and will actually grade you down on it.

13) Do not switch sides in your reply merely to agree with a board member

Frequently, a member will take a contrary position merely to draw you out and to see if you are willing and able to defend your point of view. Do not start a debate, yet do not surrender a good position. If a position is worth taking, it is worth defending.

14) Do not be afraid to admit an error in judgment if you are shown to be wrong

The board knows that you are forced to reply without any opportunity for careful consideration. Your answer may be demonstrably wrong. If so, admit it and get on with the interview.

15) Do not dwell at length on your present job

The opening question may relate to your present assignment. Answer the question but do not go into an extended discussion. You are being examined for a *new* job, not your present one. As a matter of fact, try to phrase ALL your answers in terms of the job for which you are being examined.

Basis of Rating

Probably you will forget most of these "do's" and "don'ts" when you walk into the oral interview room. Even remembering them all will not ensure you a passing grade. Perhaps you did not have the qualifications in the first place. But remembering them will help you to put your best foot forward, without treading on the toes of the board members.

Rumor and popular opinion to the contrary notwithstanding, an oral board wants you to make the best appearance possible. They know you are under pressure – but they also want to see how you respond to it as a guide to what your reaction would be under the pressures of the job you seek. They will be influenced by the degree of poise you display, the personal traits you show and the manner in which you respond.

ABOUT THIS BOOK

This book contains tests divided into Examination Sections. Go through each test, answering every question in the margin. We have also attached a sample answer sheet at the back of the book that can be removed and used. At the end of each test look at the answer key and check your answers. On the ones you got wrong, look at the right answer choice and learn. Do not fill in the answers first. Do not memorize the questions and answers, but understand the answer and principles involved. On your test, the questions will likely be different from the samples. Questions are changed and new ones added. If you understand these past questions you should have success with any changes that arise. Tests may consist of several types of questions. We have additional books on each subject should more study be advisable or necessary for you. Finally, the more you study, the better prepared you will be. This book is intended to be the last thing you study before you walk into the examination room. Prior study of relevant texts is also recommended. NLC publishes some of these in our Fundamental Series. Knowledge and good sense are important factors in passing your exam. Good luck also helps. So now study this Passbook, absorb the material contained within and take that knowledge into the examination. Then do your best to pass that exam.

EXAMINATION SECTION

EXAMINATION SECTION
TEST 1

DIRECTIONS: Each question or incomplete statement is followed by several suggested answers or completions. Select the one that BEST answers the question or completes the statement. *PRINT THE LETTER OF THE CORRECT ANSWER IN THE SPACE AT THE RIGHT.*

1. The one of the following metals which would commonly be classified as a ferrous metal is   1._____
   A. steel   B. duralumin   C. tin   D. zinc

2. To lay out an ellipse, it is USUALLY necessary to know the dimension of   2._____
   A. a radius and included angle
   B. a chord and a diagonal
   C. a diagonal and a radius
   D. the major and minor axes

3. A U.S. Standard Gauge thickness is given as 0.15625. This thickness, in fractions of an inch, is MOST NEARLY _____ inches.   3._____
   A. 1/8   B. 4/32   C. 5/32   D. 3/64

4. The weight per 100, of sheet metal fasteners, is given as 2/3 pound. The APPROXIMATE number of fasteners in a 2-pound package is   4._____
   A. 166   B. 200   C. 300   D. 266

5. The type of bolts generally used in sheet metal work are _____ bolts.   5._____
   A. stove   B. carriage   C. machine   D. expansion

6. It is desired to join two mild steel shafts with rivets. The rivet MOST generally used would be made of   6._____
   A. aluminum   B. mild steel
   C. tinned iron   D. brass

7. The size of tinner's rivets is USUALLY given on the basis of the   7._____
   A. diameter of rivet head   B. weight of 100 rivets
   C. weight of 1000 rivets   D. type of rivet shank

8. Bench or floor type drill presses can be used for   8._____
   A. crimping or beading
   B. reaming, boring, and spot facing
   C. turning or folding
   D. slitting and notching

9. To secure work to a drill press table, one should use   9._____
   A. step blocks, bolts, and clamps
   B. clamps but never step blocks
   C. magnetic chucks wired in series
   D. hand vises

10. The one of the following groupings which contains the names of four common types of metal cutting chisels is

    A. cold, cape, diamond, half round
    B. flat, diamond, half square, cross-cut
    C. diamond, caulking, cross-cut, full round
    D. half round, diamond, cross-cut, quarter round

11. A hammer GENERALLY used to flatten tinner's rivets on ducts, aside from a tinner's riveting hammer, is the type called

    A. brass-head   B. cross-peen
    C. setting   D. ball-peen

12. A common characteristic of the more generally used twist drills is that these USUALLY

    A. are square shanked
    B. have flutes milled at 20 degrees
    C. have a neck section
    D. have two cutting edges

13. Of the following, the machine generally used to shape cylinders of various diameters is a

    A. forming machine   B. bar folder
    C. turning machine   D. hand brake

14. Of the following, the tool generally used to cut a number of large round holes in sheet metal is a _____ punch.

    A. hollow   B. solid
    C. tinner's hand   D. iron hand

15. When soldering stainless stell, the flux GENERALLY used is

    A. borax   B. rosin
    C. muriatic acid   D. stearine

16. Good sheet metal practice in making a round pail requires that a(n)

    A. turning machine be used to turn the edge on the body
    B. burring machine need not be used
    C. ball peen hammer be used to bend over the double seam
    D. allowance of 1/2 inch at the bottom of pattern be made for double seaming

17. BEST sheet metal practice in making a funnel requires that

    A. a hand snip be used to cut wire
    B. the funnel spout be soldered usually on the inside of the funnel
    C. a mallet must be used to form the funnel over a stake
    D. the spout pattern corners be notched and clipped for the wired edge

18. Bench shears make the cutting of heavy gauge metal relatively easy because of the

    A. leverage obtained from the long handle and fulcrum
    B. hardened blades
    C. cropper holes
    D. small blade angle that is used

19. A corner bracket with a rounded corner is to be made. 19.____
In order to avoid tool marks when bending the piece, one should

   A. strike the metal as close to the vise as possible
   B. use a ball-peen hammer
   C. overlap the blows
   D. use soft vise clamps

20. A piece of sheetmetal has been properly cut and is to be formed into the frustrum of a 20.____
cone.
A tool MOST likely to be used in this work will be a

   A. hatchet stake   B. folding bar
   C. half moon stake   D. funnel stake

21. The one of the following considerations in connection with selection of seams which is 21.____
MOST NEARLY correct is that

   A. simple lap seams are used for metal roofing
   B. the stress and strain that seams must withstand is not important
   C. double edged seams are used to reinforce the strength of sheet metal forms
   D. grooved seams are not used to splice flat pieces

22. Several faults in drilling and reasons for them are listed below. 22.____
The one of the following statements which is MOST NEARLY correct is that:

   A. If a drill will not cut, there is too much clearance on the lips
   B. If a drill breaks, the feed was possibly too low
   C. If the corners of the drill wear away, the periphery speed is too great
   D. To avoid difficulty in drilling thin metal, do not use a flat spear pointed drill

23. The one of the following statements regarding the operating speed of drills which is 23.____
MOST NEARLY correct is that:

   A. Carbon drills should be run faster when drilling steel than iron
   B. Large size drills should be run slower than smaller ones
   C. Drill speeds for iron and steel can be greater than for brass or aluminum
   D. The drill speed depends only on the size of the drill and the metal being drilled S

24. Other conditions being proper, a satisfactory soldering job, using soft solder, will GEN- 24.____
ERALLY result if the

   A. proper flux and proper length of soldering iron are used
   B. soldering iron is lightly tinned
   C. soldering iron is of proper weight and heated red hot
   D. proper weight of soldering iron and good tinning are used

25. A piece to be rolled into semi-circular shape is to be cut from a 3 foot wide sheet. 25.____
If the radius of this shape is to be 1 foot 6 inches, the LEAST length of the material to
be cut for this purpose is MOST NEARLY _____ feet.

   A. 4.75°   B. 5.00°   C. 6.25°   D. 5.50°

26. Using a simple semicircular protractor, from a point on a base line, you are to lay out an angle of 236 degrees. This can be done by a measured angle on this protractor of MOST NEARLY

    A. 145　　　　B. 135　　　　C. 125　　　　D. 115

27. A sheet metal box is to be fabricated to hold 28 gallons of a liquid. It is known that 231 cubic inches will hold 1 gallon of this liquid.
    If the box is to be 20 inches wide and 20 inches long, then the depth should be MOST NEARLY _____ inches.

    A. 18　　　　B. 16　　　　C. 14　　　　D. 12

28. To connect a square pipe or duct to a round one in a straight line, the

    A. triangulation method of pattern development is used
    B. transition piece needs only three triangular areas
    C. taper of the sides does not have to come to a point
    D. length of the connecting piece should be at least six times the diameter of the pipe or duct

29. The slant height measurement of a right cone is always

    A. 1/2 the altitude
    B. equal to the base
    C. greater than the altitude
    D. three times the diameter of the base

30. The parallel line development method CANNOT be used to lay out

    A. elbows　　　　　　　　B. funnels
    C. ventilation pipes　　　D. hoods

31. A right triangular metal sheet for a roofing job has sides of 36 inches and 4 feet. The length of the remaining side is MOST NEARLY

    A. 7 feet　　　B. 6 feet　　　C. 60 inches　　　D. 90 inches

32. To bisect an acute angle using dividers, you would have to scribe AT LEAST _____ arc(s).

    A. 1　　　　B. 2　　　　C. 3　　　　D. 4

33. To construct a 90 degree angle without using a steel square, you would need to use

    A. dividers and straight edge
    B. hermaphrodite calipers and vernier scale
    C. inside calipers and micrometer
    D. slide calipers

34. In the phrase, *the cutting plane line is used to locate, on the drawing,* the words *cutting plane* mean MOST NEARLY

    A. section　　　　　　B. elevation
    C. visible surface　　D. dimension

35. The next section of the main duct is put up, fitted, loose flanges secured, and finally wired in position. This sentence means that

    A. the duct is first wired before securing flanges
    B. the duct is preformed
    C. the flanges are attached after the duct is readied
    D. a loose fit is required

36. In sheet metal work, the term *tolerance* means MOST NEARLY

    A. the amount of allowable variation in dimensions
    B. a necessary clearance
    C. an allowance for temperature variation of soldering irons
    D. the allowable change in fabrication due to inaccuracies of layout

37. A piece of sheet metal 2 ft. by 4 ft. is to be fabricated into a rectangular box 6 inches deep.
    Based on the use of a butt joint at the corners, the following amount of sheet metal waste will occur:

    A. 1 sq.ft.   B. 24 sq.in.   C. 48 sq.in.   D. 2 sq.ft.

38. The one of the following procedures which should be used for locating where a hole is to be drilled is to

    A. first cover the sheet metal with protective coating
    B. strike the punch with a single hard blow with a hammer
    C. use a 90 degree point after using a dot punch
    D. use a blunt scriber and a hard blow with a hammer

39. The instrument USUALLY used to lay out a large arc of greater than 15 inch radius is

    A. a bow compass
    B. a swinging blade protractor
    C. an inside caliper
    D. trammel points

40. Three basic types of calipers classified according to the method used for holding the legs in a set position are as follows: the lock joint, the firm joint, and the _____ type.

    A. vernier   B. outside
    C. inside   D. spring-bow

41. When constructing cylinders of small diameter, the type of seam generally used is the _____ seam.

    A. folded   B. simple lap
    C. double edged   D. double hemmed

42. When reading a blueprint or other drawing, it is GENERALLY found, with reference to the lines, that

    A. short dashes indicate centerlines
    B. thin long chain (dot-dash) lines indicate cutting planes
    C. zig zag lines indicate break lines
    D. short thin chain lines are used for dimensions

43. Two identical sheet metal cylinders are to be fabricated for joining at right angles. The flat sheet when laid out for each part will have

    A. 4 straight sides
    B. 2 straight and 2 curved sides
    C. 3 straight and 1 curved side
    D. 5 straight sides

44. To prepare a flux known as *cut* or *killed* acid, the acid GENERALLY used is _____ acid.

    A. sulphuric   B. muriatic
    C. hydrofluoric   D. acetic

45. A measurement on a one inch micrometer caliper shows a reading of 3 lines beyond the number 1 on the sleeve or barrel and the 4 on the thimble (having 25 divisions) lines up with horizontal or axial line on the sleeve or barrel.
    The reading is

    A. .169   B. .174   C. .179   D. .184

46. If the adjustment screw of a micrometer has a pitch of 40 threads per inch, two complete turns would change the reading MOST NEARLY _____ inches.

    A. 0.03   B. 0.05   C. 0.08   D. 0.110

47. An orthogonal projection of a right circular cone in an upright position would show a _____ as its _____.

    A. circle; front elevation
    B. triangle; plan view
    C. circle; side elevation
    D. triangle; side elevation

48. As isometric drawing of a sheet metal structure will in GENERAL

    A. show an article in a realistic manner
    B. show two sides of the article
    C. not be used for freehand sketches
    D. show horizontal lines in a horizontal position on the drawing

49. A collar gauge will COMMONLY be used on a drill to

    A. avoid use of a pilot hole
    B. correct for inaccurate center punching
    C. drill a number of holes to a given depth
    D. increase the effective size of the drill

50. When bending heavy gage metal on a cornice brake,

    A. the machine is generally operated very slowly
    B. a reinforcing bar is generally used on the bending leaf
    C. extra clamping handles are used
    D. forming molds are usually used

KEY (CORRECT ANSWERS)

1. A	11. B	21. C	31. C	41. B
2. D	12. D	22. C	32. C	42. C
3. C	13. A	23. B	33. A	43. C
4. C	14. A	24. D	34. A	44. B
5. A	15. C	25. A	35. C	45. C
6. B	16. A	26. C	36. A	46. B
7. C	17. D	27. B	37. A	47. D
8. B	18. A	28. A	38. C	48. A
9. A	19. C	29. C	39. D	49. C
10. A	20. D	30. B	40. D	50. B

TEST 2

DIRECTIONS: Each question or incomplete statement is followed by several suggested answers or completions. Select the one that BEST answers the question or completes the statement. *PRINT THE LETTER OF THE CORRECT ANSWER IN THE SPACE AT THE RIGHT.*

1. Two lengths of galvanized sheet iron pipes each 4" in diameter by 36" long with a 1/4" groove seam are to be joined.
   The one of the following groupings of tools which would be among those used is

   A. squaring shears, crimping machine, pipe folder, forming machine
   B. pipe folder, forming machine, squaring shears, double seaming machine
   C. crimping machine, pipe folder, squaring shears, burring machine
   D. pipe folder, crimping machine, squaring shears, cornice brake

   1.____

2. The one of the following features which CANNOT be adjusted on the common type of folding machine is

   A. shoe
   B. folded edge width
   C. metal thickness adjustment
   D. folded edge sharpness

   2.____

3. The one of the following components which is NOT a basic part of common bench stakes is

   A. horn   B. head   C. neck   D. shank

   3.____

4. The tool used to cut extra heavy gage sheet metal is called a

   A. double cutting shears   B. bench shears
   C. bulldog snips   D. combination snips

   4.____

5. To form a round edge using a bar folder, it is necessary to

   A. adjust the gage adjusting screw
   B. adjust the adjustable collar
   C. lower the wing
   D. set the stops

   5.____

6. Two pieces of sheet metal each 3 ft. wide are to be joined by a hooked joint. Four inches on each sheet are used in the making of the entire hook.
   When joining, the overall width of the joined sheets will MOST NEARLY be 5 ft. _____ in.

   A. 4   B. 6   C. 2   D. 8

   6.____

7. If two sheet metal pipes of equal diameter are to be fitted into each other, the end of the male pipe in this joint is prepared in a _____ machine.

   A. crimping   B. beading   C. forming   D. grooving

   7.____

8. The amount of material allowance USUALLY added for the grooved seam lock is NOT less than _____ times the width of the lock.   8.____

   A. 2   B. 3   C. 4   D. 5

9. The operation of wiring in sheet metal work   9.____

   A. is limited to flat sections
   B. eliminates the raw edges of sheet metal
   C. is entirely a hand operation
   D. is done in a cornice brake

10. A standing seam used as a cross seam on a large duct   10.____

    A. eliminates the need for angle iron reinforcement
    B. is the most difficult seam to make
    C. is used when a flat surface is required
    D. is used mainly for light gage metal

11. An easy and convenient method for joining a sheet metal collar to a flange is to use a _____ seam.   11.____

    A. handy   B. slip joint
    C. cap strip   D. dove tail

12. To fabricate a large double-seamed corner, the one of the following machines which is GENERALLY used is a   12.____

    A. bar folder   B. turning machine
    C. grooving machine   D. cornice brake

13. A general guide to use in determining the size of a rivet to use for plates is that the rivet diameter   13.____

    A. should be 2 times the plate thickness
    B. equal the plate thickness
    C. should be 4 times the plate thickness
    D. should be about 1 1/2 times the thickness of plates to be riveted

14. The two standard lap joints for riveting aluminum and its alloys are _____ joints.   14.____

    A. lap and butt   B. lap and seam
    C. butt and seam   D. end and overlay

15. The one of the following which is NOT a standard screw-nail head style is   15.____

    A. plain flat   B. counter sunk flat
    C. large round   D. counter sunk oval

16. When soldering a lap seam,   16.____

    A. the iron is held at an angle of 30 degrees with flat point across the seam
    B. use a short stroke of the copper
    C. move the copper slowly for sweating of the full width of the seam
    D. apply solder to the copper before soldering the seam

17. To keep the tinned part of the soldering copper bright and clean,

    A. a woolen wiping rag is preferred
    B. a dipping solution of zinc chloride is usually used
    C. dip a hot copper into a sal ammoniac solution
    D. wire brush the copper frequently

18. The flux commonly used for soldering iron or steel is

    A. rosin   B. zinc chloride
    C. borax   D. tallow

19. In the phrase, *to planish a cylindrical surface,* the word *planish* means MOST NEARLY

    A. toughen by hammering   B. polish by chemicals
    C. soften by annealing   D. clean by using an acid

20. In the phrase, *laying out holes for longitudinal seams,* the word *longitudinal* means MOST NEARLY

    A. lateral   B. lengthwise
    C. transverse   D. axial

21. When a metal is annealed, the process will NOT

    A. restore the ductility
    B. relieve the internal stresses
    C. restore the elasticity
    D. affect the grain size

22. To MOST accurately measure the diameter of a small rod, the one of the following devices which should be used is a

    A. combination square with centering head
    B. circumference rule
    C. pocket slide caliper
    D. hermaphrodite caliper

23. A sheet of iron approximately 5/16 inches in thickness is USUALLY designated by the following gauge:

    A. U.S. Standard 0.3125
    B. Wire Gauge #0
    C. Brown & Sharpe 0.32486
    D. American S & W Co. 0.009

24. The one of the following which is characteristic of sheet metal screws is that

    A. the driving tips are blunted
    B. the sheet metal screws are not made with hex heads
    C. the threads extend over the entire length
    D. they are made in a very limited number of sizes

25. In preparing to lay out a pattern on metal, the one of FIRST steps is to square the corners of the sheet since   25.____

    A. layouts must be made from two edges
    B. patterns have straight edges
    C. straight lines on patterns are at right angles to each other
    D. sheet metal is not squared true before leaving the factory

26. If two metal sheets of U.S. Standard Gage 18 and 24, respectively, are compared, it will be found that the   26.____

    A. 24 gage is about twice as heavy as the 18 gage
    B. 24 gage is .024 inch thick and the 18 gage is .018 inch thick
    C. 18 gage is about three times as heavy as the 24 gage
    D. 18 gage is about twice as thick as the 24 gage

27. An object having a hexagon shape is to be laid out in sheet metal. When completed, the   27.____

    A. figure will have 8 sides
    B. angle between any two adjacent lines will be 120
    C. figure will have 5 sides
    D. the angle between any two adjacent lines will be 60

28. A *dead-soft* steel sheet would   28.____

    A. be ductile and malleable
    B. be highly elastic
    C. have a high Rockwell Hardness Test number
    D. not have same basic characteristics as galvanized iron

29. To produce a matting finish on metal, one should   29.____

    A. apply a few drops of oil on fine grain emery and rub the metal briskly
    B. rub the surface with a coarse bristle brush that has been dipped into a pumice and water mixture
    C. use chemical solutions
    D. use a punch and hammer

30. A 10-inch file is one which is 10" in length from the end to _____ of the tang   30.____

    A. the tip
    B. base
    C. middle
    D. a point one inch below the base

KEY (CORRECT ANSWERS)

1.	A	11.	D	21.	C
2.	A	12.	D	22.	C
3.	C	13.	D	23.	A
4.	B	14.	A	24.	C
5.	C	15.	D	25.	D
6.	B	16.	C	26.	D
7.	A	17.	C	27.	B
8.	B	18.	C	28.	A
9.	B	19.	A	29.	D
10.	A	20.	B	30.	B

EXAMINATION SECTION
TEST 1

DIRECTIONS: Each question or incomplete statement is followed by several suggested answers or completions. Select the one that BEST answers the question or completes the statement. *PRINT THE LETTER OF THE CORRECT ANSWER IN THE SPACE AT THE RIGHT.*

1. Killed acid is   1.____

    A. zinc sulphate
    C. copper chloride
    B. copper sulphate
    D. zinc chloride

2. Heat for brazing is NOT applied by a   2.____

    A. charcoal fire
    C. soldering iron
    B. gasoline torch
    D. gas torch

3. For expanding a ring from 4 inches to 6 inches diameter, the tool that should be used is   3.____

    A. cone mandrel
    C. hardie
    B. fuller
    D. punch

4. A fold to receive a wire is known as a(n) _____ lock.   4.____

    A. closed   B. open   C. sharp   D. double

5. Terne plate is   5.____

    A. sheet tin
    B. burnished alloy steel sheet
    C. copper bearing sheet steel
    D. tin and lead plated sheet steel

6. Sheet galvanized iron is USUALLY made of   6.____

    A. hot zinc rolled into hot iron
    B. sheet iron coated with zinc by electroplating
    C. sheet iron dipped in melted zinc
    D. sheet iron covered with zinc by galvanic action

7. A drive cleat is used   7.____

    A. as a duct cross seam
    B. as a wedge for tightening standing seams
    C. as part of flashing
    D. in closing box corner seams

8. A main duct 20 inches in diameter discharges into two branch ducts. The sum of the areas of the branches is to be equal to the area of the main duct. One branch is 12 inches in diameter.   8.____
   The diameter of the other branch is _____ inches.

    A. 16   B. 12   C. 10   D. 8

9. For soldering copper, the BEST flux is

   A. cut acid
   B. sal ammoniac
   C. muriatic acid
   D. borax

10. An ogee is

    A. a quarter round moulding
    B. used on rectangular ducts
    C. a bench
    D. an *S* curve

11. Carburizing is a process of

    A. pickling
    B. tempering
    C. case hardening
    D. annealing

12. The parallel line method should be used in developing the pattern for a

    A. two-piece 45 round elbow
    B. reducing elbow
    C. wedge
    D. fission piece

13. Forming rolls for sheet metal are USUALLY used to make

    A. cylinders
    B. rolled seams
    C. mouldings
    D. warped surfaces

14. Solder for sheet metal is composed of

    A. zinc and tin
    B. tin and lead
    C. zinc and lead
    D. zinc, lead, and tin

15. A crimping machine is used to

    A. make some forms of roofing
    B. crease seams
    C. make throats of round section elbows
    D. shrink ends of cylinders T

16. If work is forged by *upsetting*, the piece is

    A. bent
    B. lengthened
    C. shortened
    D. straightened

17. Brass is an alloy PRINCIPALLY of

    A. copper, tin, and nickel
    B. copper and tin with a small amount of zinc
    C. copper and tin
    D. copper and zinc

18. A finial is

    A. used in tracing irregular curves
    B. the bottom part of a skylight
    C. a roof ornament
    D. an architectural support for a cornice

19. A box-finger would be found on a

    A. grooving machine   B. brace
    C. bar folder   D. stake

20. The area, in square inches, of a right triangle that has sides of 12 1/2, 10, and 7 1/2 inches is

    A. 18 1/4   B. 37 1/2   C. 75   D. 60

21. An open lock is a

    A. seam that is to be soldered
    B. roofing tool
    C. part of a seam that is unfinished
    D. flat fold

22. The bond of a brazed joint is USUALLY made with a mixture of

    A. zinc and antimony   B. copper and lead
    C. copper and zinc   D. copper and antimony

23. A transition piece is used

    A. to join round ducts that are off-center
    B. to join a smaller to a larger duct
    C. in bringing a duct through a wall
    D. to join a square duct to a rectangular duct

24. The shape of the end of a *bottom* soldering iron is that of a

    A. pyramid   B. cone   C. square   D. wedge

25. In forge welding, the BEST flux is

    A. alum and borax   B. borax and sal ammoniac
    C. rosin and borax   D. sand and rosin

26. A blowhorn stake is used to make

    A. funnels   B. stove pipe
    C. small tubes   D. raised surfaces

27. A steep tin roof should be attached to the wooden roof supporting it by nailing

    A. only at roof peak
    B. under edges of sheet forming the seam
    C. short pieces that are folded into the seam
    D. directly and soldering over the nailheads t

28. For steep roofs, the MOST advisable method of joining tin sheets is by _____ horizontal and _____ seams.

    A. flat; vertical
    B. standing; vertical
    C. flat; standing vertical
    D. standing; flat vertical

29. A plenum is a

    A. type of cornice
    B. tool for working sheet metal
    C. part of a ventilation system
    D. forging tool

30. A condensation gutter is found in

    A. skylights
    B. tin and corrugated iron roofing
    C. air conditioning ducts
    D. air washers

31. From a sheet 24 inches by 72 inches, a piece is cut to the drawing shown at the right. The waste, in square inches, is
    A. 464
    B. 374
    C. 298
    D. 86

32. To temper a cold chisel, the PROPER procedure is to

    A. heat to a cherry red and quench
    B. cool to a straw color and quench
    C. heat to a light straw color
    D. heat to a purple color

33. The appearance of steel at the proper forge welding temperature is

    A. yellowish white
    B. bright white
    C. cherry red
    D. cherry yellow

34. Borax is USUALLY used as a flux for soldering

    A. tin
    B. zinc
    C. galvanized iron
    D. brass

35. A round reducer approximately 4 feet long is to be used to join a 36-inch diameter duct to a 30-inch diameter duct that is out of line by 10 inches.
    The MOST practicable method of developing the pattern is by

    A. triangulation
    B. parallel line
    C. radial line
    D. second angle perspective

36. If steel weighs 480 lbs. per cubic foot, the weight of 10 sheets, each 6 feet by 3 feet by 1/32 inch, is _____ lbs.

    A. 2700
    B. 1237
    C. 270
    D. 225

37. The BEST machine for forming sheets into moulding shapes is the 37.____

   A. bar folder
   B. cornice brake
   C. forming machine
   D. slip roll

38. The length of 1 inch diameter round stock required to make a 6-inch inside diameter ring is _____ inches. 38.____

   A. 19
   B. 22
   C. 24
   D. 25 1/8

39. The SMALLEST diameter stake is a 39.____

   A. needle case
   B. conductor
   C. beak horn
   D. candle mold

40. The Pittsburgh lock seam is used 40.____

   A. on round ducts
   B. on 3-piece 90° round elbows
   C. in the side of rectangular ducts
   D. on the corners of rectangular ducts

KEY (CORRECT ANSWERS)

1. D	11. C	21. C	31. B
2. C	12. A	22. C	32. D
3. A	13. A	23. D	33. A
4. B	14. B	24. D	34. D
5. D	15. D	25. B	35. A
6. C	16. C	26. A	36. D
7. A	17. D	27. C	37. B
8. A	18. C	28. C	38. B
9. A	19. B	29. C	39. A
10. D	20. B	30. A	40. D

TEST 2

DIRECTIONS: Each question or incomplete statement is followed by several suggested answers or completions. Select the one that BEST answers the question or completes the statement. *PRINT THE LETTER OF THE CORRECT ANSWER IN THE SPACE AT THE RIGHT.*

1. A hold down is used on a 1.____
   - A. crimper
   - B. circular shears
   - C. lever slitting shears
   - D. squaring shears

2. After forging, the CORRECT treatment for a crowbar is 2.____
   - A. annealing
   - B. tempering
   - C. hardening
   - D. none

3. For preparing a curved edge for wiring, there should be used a 3.____
   - A. grooving horn
   - B. creasing stake
   - C. wiring horn
   - D. hardie

4. When mild steel is at the proper temperature for forging, it is 4.____
   - A. cherry red
   - B. creamy yellow
   - C. white hot
   - D. bluish red

5. In making a container to hold 1 gallon (231 cu.in.) and to be 6 inches in diameter at the top and 8 inches in diameter at the bottom, the height must be, in inches, 5.____
   - A. 10.0
   - B. 8.2
   - C. 4.6
   - D. 6

6. The width of material, in inches, for a 7-inch diameter 20-gage pipe with 3/8-inch pipe seam is 6.____
   - A. 21
   - B. 22 3/8
   - C. 23 1/8
   - D. 24 3/8

7. For seaming cylinders, the BEST machine is a 7.____
   - A. brake
   - B. pipe folder
   - C. bar folder
   - D. double seamer

8. Swages are used for 8.____
   - A. splitting
   - B. tapering
   - C. making square corners
   - D. round work

9. When attaching copper roofing, there should be used 9.____
   - A. galvanized iron nails
   - B. wire nails with lead washers
   - C. copper nails
   - D. galvanized nails with copper washers

10. For raising a seam on a pipe, it should be placed on a 10.____
    - A. grooving horn
    - B. blowhorn stake
    - C. slip roll
    - D. hemmer

11. If a forged piece, after cooling, is cracked on the inside, it has been   11.____

    A. heated too fast
    B. heated too slowly
    C. forged while too hot on the inside
    D. forged while too cold on the outside

12. For a forge lap weld, the ends should be   12.____

    A. flattened   B. upset and scarfed
    C. scarfed   D. point and vee

13. Roofing with tin where the roof pitch is small should be done with _____ horizontal and   13.____
    _____ seams.

    A. flat; vertical   B. standing; vertical
    C. flat; standing vertical   D. standing; flat vertical

14. In preparing pieces for butt welding, the ends should be   14.____

    A. slightly rounded
    B. scarfed
    C. squared off
    D. pointed on one and vee shaped on the other

15. When steel has been slightly overheated, the BEST treatment is to   15.____

    A. work it lightly at low heat
    B. cool it quickly and normalize
    C. quench in oil and reheat
    D. let it cool slowly and anneal

16. A flux is used in forge welding PRIMARILY to   16.____

    A. lower the melting point of the steel
    B. lower the melting point of the scale
    C. burn off the scale
    D. crack off the scale

17. A clinch collar is used to   17.____

    A. connect a square duct to the side of a square duct
    B. hold a pipe while it is being seamed
    C. flash a pipe that goes through a roof
    D. join a round duct into the side of a round duct

18. Tempering   18.____

    A. makes the grain smaller
    B. increases thstrength
    C. makes the piece brittle
    D. softens the piece

19. A hardie is used for   19._____
    A. forming fillets
    B. finishing square corners
    C. cutting off
    D. working with curved pieces

20. The BEST coal for smithing purposes is a   20._____
    A. hard coal
    B. coal high in sulphur
    C. soft coking coal
    D. low volatile coal

21. The name of the HEAVIEST stake is   21._____
    A. bottom
    B. hollow mandrel
    C. bathtub
    D. conductor

22. The machine that is USUALLY used to strengthen stove pipe against becoming oval is the   22._____
    A. beading rolls
    B. crimping machine
    C. burring machine
    D. groover

Questions 23-40.

DIRECTIONS: For Questions 23 through 40, inclusive, the item is given in Column I. You are to select the BEST answer in Column II.

Questions 23-24.

COLUMN I	COLUMN II	
23. The shape of the peening head of a raising hammer	A. Conical B. Wedge C. Mushroom D. Cylindrical E. Flat round F. Ball	23._____
24. The shape of the peening head of a setting down hammer		24._____

Questions 25-30.

DIRECTIONS: Questions 25 through 30 show sketches of sheet metal joints or seams. Select from Column II the name usually used for each item.

COLUMN I

25. [figure]

26. [figure]

27. [figure]

COLUMN II

A. Philadelphia lock
B. Slip
C. Double corner lock
D. Lap seam
E. Double hem
F. Drive cleat
G. Pittsburgh lock
H. Double seam

25. ____
26. ____
27. ____

COLUMN I

28. [figure]

29. [figure]

30. [figure]

COLUMN II

I. Cross single lock
J. Grooved seam
K. Standing seam
L. Flat lock seam
M. Box seam
N. Standing double seam
O. Rigid slip

28. ____
29. ____
30. ____

Questions 31-34.

DIRECTIONS: For Questions 31 through 34, inclusive, use the sketch below of a plan view of a skylight.

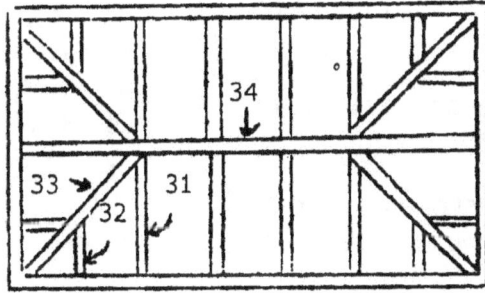

COLUMN I

31. Piece numbered 31
32. Piece numbered 32
33. Piece numbered 33
34. Piece numbered 34

COLUMN II

A. Hip bar
B. Side bar
C. King bar
D. Center bar
E. Jack bar
F. Common bar
G. Roof bar
H. Angle bar
I. Hitch bar
J. Curb bar

31. ____
32. ____
33. ____
34. ____

Questions 35-40.

DIRECTIONS: Questions 35 through 40, inclusive, are to be answered on the basis of the cutaway sketch shown below. For each item in Column I, you are to select the CORRECT answer from Column II.

CUTAWAY SKETCH OF A CONTAINER

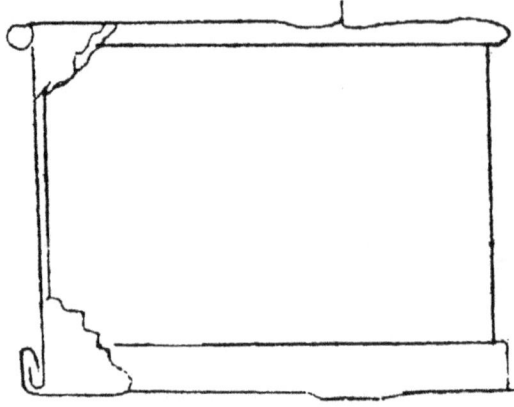

COLUMN I

35. For the third (that is the last) operation in making the bottom joint, use the

36. For the second operation in making the bottom joint, use the

37. For the first operation in making the bottom joint, use the

38. For the last operation on the sheet in making the wired edge, use the

39. For the next to the last operation on the sheet in making the wired edge, use the

40. For the preparation of the wire for the wired edge, use a

COLUMN II

A. Beading rolls
B. Burring machine
C. Circular grooving
D. Forming rolls
E. Double seamer
F. Turning machine
G. Standard seamer
H. Setting down machine
I. Moulding brake
J. Rotary folder
K. Wiring machine
L. Crimping machine
M. Single hammer
N. Groover
O. Bar folder

35.____
36.____
37.____
38.____
39.____
40.____

KEY (CORRECT ANSWERS)

1. D	11. D	21. B	31. F
2. D	12. B	22. A	32. E
3. B	13. A	23. C	33. A
4. A	14. A	24. B	34. D
5. D	15. D	25. G	35. E
6. C	16. B	26. H	36. H
7. B	17. A	27. J	37. B
8. D	18. D	28. D	38. K
9. C	19. C	29. B	39. F
10. A	20. C	30. F	40. D

EXAMINATION SECTION
TEST 1

DIRECTIONS: Each question or incomplete statement is followed by several suggested answers or completions. Select the one that BEST answers the question or completes the statement. *PRINT THE LETTER OF THE CORRECT ANSWER IN THE SPACE AT THE RIGHT.*

1. The hole diameter required for a 1 lb. tinners' rivet is MOST NEARLY   1.____

   A. 1/16"   B. 1/8"   C. 3/16"   D. 1/4"

Questions 2-3.

DIRECTIONS: Questions 2 and 3 refer to the sketch of the pipe shown below.

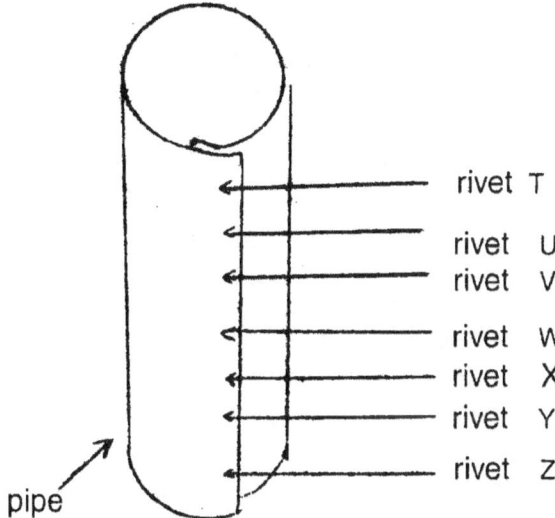

2. In riveting the seam shown above, the FIRST set of rivets that should be inserted in their holes is the set of rivets   2.____

   A. T and Z   B. U and Y   C. T and Y   D. U and Z

3. In riveting the seam shown above, the FIRST rivet that should be completely headed is rivet   3.____

   A. T   B. Z   C. U   D. W

4. Fire dampers in ductwork are generally held open by   4.____

   A. cotter pins   B. fusible links
   C. double-throw switches   D. coiled springs

25

5.

clearance space

The sketch shown above represents a sheet metal corner lap seam.
The space that should be allowed for clearance when using 26 gage sheet metal is MOST NEARLY

   A. 7/16"   B. 5/16"   C. 3/16"   D. 1/16"

6. The MAIN reason for wiring the top edge of a large sheet metal can is to
   A. decrease the expansion of the can due to heat
   B. improve the appearance of the can
   C. increase the strength of the top of the can
   D. make it easier to form the rolled edge of the can

7. Short sections of pipe used to change the direction of ductwork in heating systems are known as
   A. tailpieces   B. fittings
   C. headpieces   D. neckpieces

8. Of the following tinners' rivet sizes, the one that should be used to rivet together two sheets of 26-gage sheet metal is _____ lb.
   A. 1   B. 2   C. 2 1/2   D. 3

9. Of the following types of seams, the one that is a dovetailed seam used in sheet metal work is the _____ seam.
   A. chamfered   B. beaded   C. dadoed   D. lapped

10. The tip of a soldering iron should be covered with solder before being used. The process of applying this solder to the tip is known as
    A. capping   B. skinning   C. tipping   D. tinning

11. The corner seam shown in the sketch at the right is a
    A. Pittsburgh lock
    B. concealed lock
    C. flange dovetail
    D. beaded dovetail

12. To prevent slippage of the sheet metal, seams are MOST often locked by using a
    A. rivet punch   B. Hilti-gun
    C. center punch and hammer   D. needle-nose pliers

13. In figuring the allowance for additional sheet metal needed to make a wired edge on 26-gage sheet metal, the diameter of the wire should be multiplied by

    A. 1 1/2   B. 2 1/2   C. 3 1/2   D. 4 1/2

14. Small openings around filters, cooling coils, and heating coils are frequently closed with galvanized sheet steel. This practice is known as

    A. safing   B. sounding   C. saddling   D. dunning

15. A hold-down clamp is a part normally found on a power-driven

    A. forming machine
    C. squaring shear
    B. drill
    D. oil-stone grinder

16. The stake that should be used for hand-forming a small sheet metal cone is a _____ stake.

    A. hatchet
    C. solid mandrel
    B. bottom
    D. blowhorn

17. A connection between a sheet metal duct and a fan should USUALLY be made by means of a

    A. Dresser coupling
    C. labyrinth ring
    B. corrugated expansion joint
    D. flexible collar

18. A bench plate is MOST often used to

    A. hold stakes
    C. make moldings
    B. sharpen tools
    D. bend steel rods

19. Of the following machines, the one that should be used to form the round edge that receives the wire used for a wired edge is a _____ machine.

    A. grooving   B. turning   C. beading   D. wiring

20.

    The sheet metal bead shown in the sketch above is a(n) _____ bead.

    A. single   B. ogee   C. cavetto   D. ragel

KEY (CORRECT ANSWERS)

1.	B	11.	A
2.	A	12.	C
3.	D	13.	B
4.	B	14.	A
5.	C	15.	C
6.	C	16.	D
7.	B	17.	D
8.	A	18.	A
9.	B	19.	B
10.	D	20.	B

TEST 2

DIRECTIONS: Each question or incomplete statement is followed by several suggested answers or completions. Select the one that BEST answers the question or completes the statement. *PRINT THE LETTER OF THE CORRECT ANSWER IN THE SPACE AT THE RIGHT.*

1. Of the following, the part that must be tightened on a drill press to properly secure a straight shank drill is the 1._____

   A. chuck
   B. lock quill
   C. collar
   D. gib head

2. Of the following gage designations, the one that is used for aluminum sheet metal is 2._____

   A. W & M B. B & S C. USSG D. G & M

3. Of the following types of pliers, the BEST one to use to clamp down sheet metal to the top of a work bench is the 3._____

   A. channel-lock
   B. vise grip
   C. slip-joint
   D. duck bill

4. The CORRECT machine to use to corrugate the end of a sheet metal pipe so that it can be fitted into another sheet metal pipe of the same diameter is the _____ machine, 4._____

   A. setting down
   B. burring
   C. elbow edge
   D. crimping

5. The wall and ceiling units that distribute air into a room are known as 5._____

   A. spreaders B. diffusers C. headers D. baffles

6. Of the following, the BEST flux to use for soldering galvanized iron is 6._____

   A. raw muriatic acid
   B. rosin
   C. sal ammoniac
   D. zinc chloride

7. Angle brackets for supporting ductwork are commonly anchored to concrete walls by means of _____ bolts. 7._____

   A. carriage B. J- C. expansion D. foot

8. Of the following bolts, the one that should be used when attaching a hanger to a wooden joist is a _____ bolt. 8._____

   A. dead B. lag C. dardalet D. toggle

9. Transite hoods that are used to handle chemical exhausts are made from cement and 9._____

   A. asbestos
   B. fiberglass
   C. lucite
   D. bauxite

10. Of the following sheet metals, the one that is the MOST resistant to corrosion is 10._____

    A. copper
    B. aluminum
    C. monel
    D. galvanized steel

11. When bending sheet metal by hand, the BEST tool to use is a

    A. hand groover
    B. hand seamer
    C. hand ball tooler
    D. hand plier

12. Electric soldering irons are rated according to

    A. weight
    B. wattage
    C. length
    D. resistance

13. An example of a hand sheet metal punch is the _____ punch.

    A. Whitney
    B. revolving
    C. arch
    D. drive

14. Copper known as 16 oz. copper weighs 16 oz. per

    A. square foot
    B. square yard
    C. roofing square
    D. running foot of parapet wall

15. The melting point of half-and-half tin-lead solder is _____ the melting point of _____.

    A. greater than; tin
    B. equal to; lead
    C. less than; tin
    D. equal to one-half; lead

16. Of the following types of steel rivets of the same size, the STRONGEST is the _____ rivet.

    A. tinners'
    B. flathead
    C. roundhead
    D. countersunk

17. Of the following snips, the one that can cut relatively thick sheet metal with the LEAST effort is _____ snips.

    A. straight
    B. aviation
    C. duck bill
    D. hawk bill

18. Of the following metals, the one that expands the MOST upon being heated is

    A. steel
    B. tin
    C. copper
    D. aluminum

19. The stake shown in the sketch at the right is a _____ stake.
    A. hatchet
    B. conductor
    C. solid mandrel
    D. beak horn

20. When a circle is too large to be drawn with a pair of dividers, the PROPER tool to use is a

    A. trammel
    B. protractor
    C. combination set
    D. flexible curve

KEY (CORRECT ANSWERS)

1.	A	11.	B
2.	B	12.	B
3.	B	13.	A
4.	D	14.	A
5.	B	15.	C
6.	A	16.	C
7.	C	17.	B
8.	B	18.	D
9.	A	19.	A
10.	C	20.	A

EXAMINATION SECTION
TEST 1

DIRECTIONS: Each question or incomplete statement is followed by several suggested answers or completions. Select the one that BEST answers the question or completes the statement. *PRINT THE LETTER OF THE CORRECT ANSWER IN THE SPACE AT THE RIGHT.*

1. The one of the following which is a reason for using flux in soldering is to

    A. reduce the amount of heat required
    B. permit the use of a smaller soldering iron
    C. make the solder flow more smoothly
    D. clean the metal around the joint

    1._____

2. A rivet set is a tool used to

    A. shape the head of a rivet
    B. mark off the spacing of rivets
    C. remove a loose rivet
    D. check the shank length of a rivet

    2._____

3.

    The hammer shown in the above sketch is a _____ hammer.

    A. raising   B. ball peen   C. setting   D. cross-over

    3._____

4. Of the following, the BEST tool to use to scribe a line parallel to the straight edge of a piece of sheet metal is a(n)

    A. outside caliper   B. pair of dividers
    C. template   D. scratch gage

    4._____

5. Hardware for sheet metal shelving requires 1/4-20 1/2 bolts. The *1/2* stands for the

    A. diameter of the bolt   B. length of the bolt
    C. diameter of the head   D. pitch of the threads

    5._____

6. The QUICKEST way to draw a 25° angle is to use a

    A. pair of dividers   B. combination square
    C. protractor   D. circumference rule

    6._____

7. When laying out the centers of 6 equally-spaced holes on the circumference of a 7" diameter circle, the dividers should be set to

    A. 3 1/2"   B. 3 3/4"   C. 4"   D. 4 1/4"

    7._____

33

8. If sheets of #16 and #22 USSG sheet steel are compared for thickness, it will be found that the #22 gage sheet is MOST NEARLY _____ as thick as the #16 gage sheet.   8.____

   A. 3 times   B. twice as   C. 1/4   D. 1/2

9. Connections between steel sheet metal work and copper should be made with insulating gaskets made of   9.____

   A. rubber   B. steel   C. lead   D. copper

10. A MAJOR advantage of pop rivets is that these rivets   10.____

    A. can be set with a light hammer
    B. require no pre-drilling of rivet holes
    C. are cheaper than ordinary tinners' rivets
    D. may be installed and set from one side of the work

11. An object having a hexagonal shape is to be laid out in sheet metal. When completed, the figure will have _____ sides.   11.____

    A. 4   B. 5   C. 6   D. 7

12. Following are steps that must be taken in order to draw the pattern for an ellipse: 12.____
    I. Draw a circle whose diameter is equal to the large diameter of the ellipse
    II. Using the same center, draw a circle whose diameter is equal to the small diameter of the ellipse
    III. Divide the small circle into a number of small equal parts
    The correct NEXT step is to draw _____ lines.

    A. radial   B. tangent   C. horizontal   D. vertical

13.   13.____

                                .A

    B_____C

    It is required to draw a line through point A which will be perpendicular to line BC in the sketch shown above. The FIRST step is to

    A. draw two random lines through point A intersecting line BC
    B. draw another line through point A, parallel to line BC
    C. use point A as a center to draw an arc which intersects line BC at two points
    D. use any point on line BC as a center and draw an arc intersecting point A

14.   14.____

    TOP VIEW   FRONT VIEW

    The pattern for the transition piece shown above should be made by

    A. parallel line development   B. triangulation
    C. radial line development   D. auxiliary view development

15. Neglecting edging seam allowance, the stretchout length for a 12 1/2" inside diameter, 0.06" thick sheet metal pipe is MOST NEARLY

    A. 39 1/8"   B. 39 7/16"   C. 39 11/16"   D. 40 1/4"

16. The two patterns required for a T-joint should be made by

    A. radial line development
    B. parallel line development
    C. triangulation
    D. resection

17. Where there are no clearance problems, the layout of a 5-piece 90° elbow GENERALLY requires _____ patterns.

    A. two   B. three   C. four   D. five

18. The pattern required for a regular cone should be made by

    A. auxiliary view development
    B. parallel line development
    C. radial line development
    D. resection

19. When making a pattern for a rectangular duct, allowance should be made for joining the parts of the ductwork using which of the following?

    A. Crimped edges   B. Drive clips
    C. Dovetail seams   D. Spot welds

20. The sketch shown at the right shows the front view of a line $A_V B_V$ and the top view of the same line $A_V B_V$ in the drawing for making a pattern. The TRUE length of line AB is equal to the length of line

    A. $A_h C_h$
    B. $A_v C_v$
    C. $B_v C_v$
    D. $C_h C_v$

KEY (CORRECT ANSWERS)

1.	D	11.	C
2.	A	12.	A
3.	C	13.	C
4.	D	14.	B
5.	B	15.	B
6.	C	16.	B
7.	A	17.	A
8.	D	18.	C
9.	A	19.	B
10.	D	20.	B

TEST 2

DIRECTIONS: Each question or incomplete statement is followed by several suggested answers or completions. Select the one that BEST answers the question or completes the statement. *PRINT THE LETTER OF THE CORRECT ANSWER IN THE SPACE AT THE RIGHT.*

1. The instructions for the drawing of a pattern for a T-joint state the following: *Step off, locate, and number the element lines on the stretchout.*
   The *stepping off* is USUALLY done with

   A. a protractor   B. a square
   C. dividers   D. a circumference ruler

   1.____

2. Of the following, the FIRST step to take in preparing to lay out a pattern directly on a piece of sheet metal is to make sure that the

   A. top and bottom edges of the sheet are parallel
   B. sides of the sheet are perpendicular to each other
   C. left and right sides of the sheet are parallel
   D. sheet lays flat on the work bench

   2.____

3. A sheet metal worker is given a job to make a transition piece from an 8 1/2" diameter duct to an 11 1/4" diameter duct. If the length of the transition piece is 5 1/2" for each inch change in diameter, then the length of the transition piece is

   A. 14 7/8"   B. 15"   C. 15 1/8"   D. 15 1/4"

   3.____

4. A duct layout is drawn to a scale of 3/8" to a foot.
   If the length of a run shown on the drawing scales 7 1/2", then the ACTUAL length of the run is

   A. 19'6"   B. 19'9"   C. 20'0"   D. 20'3"

   4.____

5. An 18" x 24" duct is to be connected to a 24" x 24" duct by means of an eccentric transition piece (3 sides flush). If the taper is to be 1" in 4", then the length of the transition piece is

   A. 6"   B. 12"   C. 18"   D. 24"

   5.____

6. Twenty-seven pairs of 3/8" diameter rods each 3'3 1/2" long are needed to support a duct.
   If the available rods are ten feet long, then the MINIMUM number of rods that will be needed to make the twenty-seven sets is

   A. 9   B. 12   C. 15   D. 18

   6.____

7. A rectangular sheet metal air duct with open ends is 12 feet long and 15" x 20" in cross section. If one square foot of the sheet metal weighs 1/2 pound, then the TOTAL weight of the duct is _____ lbs.

   A. 10   B. 17 1/2   C. 35   D. 150

   7.____

37

8.
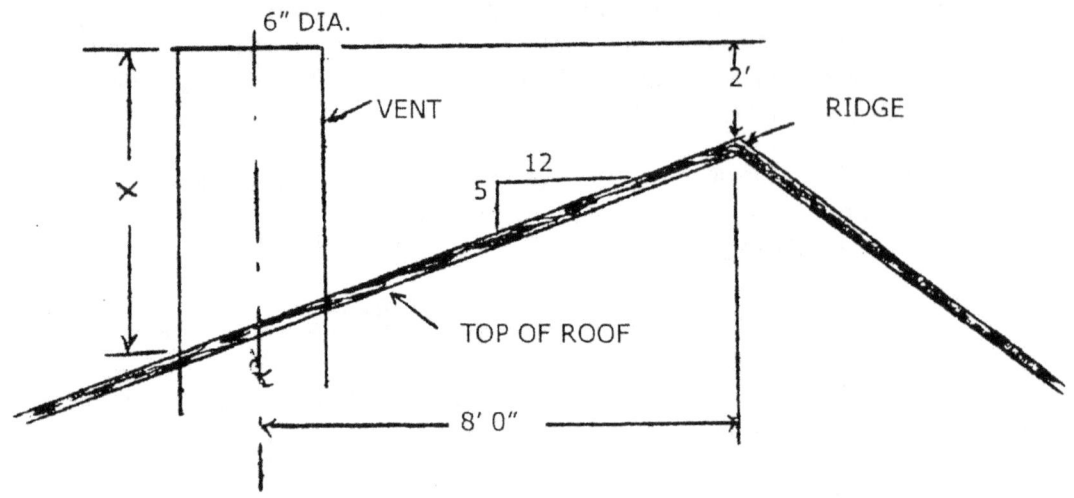

The above sketch represents a sheet metal vent going through a roof. The length X is

A. 5'2 3/4"   B. 5'4"   C. 5'5 1/4"   D. 5'6 1/2"

9.
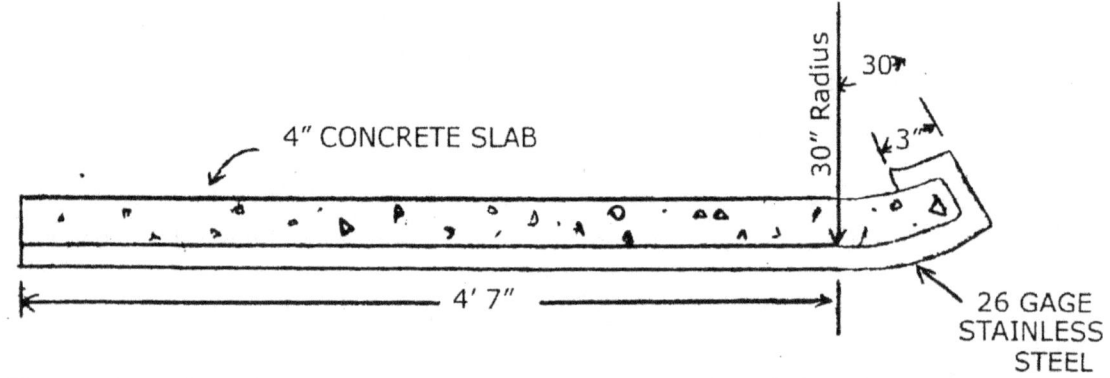

Shown above is a sketch of a concrete canopy which is to be covered with stainless steel as shown. The total length of slab to be covered is MOST NEARLY

A. 6'5 3/4"   B. 6'11 5/8"   C. 6'8 1/8"   D. 7'2"

10. The total number of 8-oz. solid flathead tin-plated tinners rivets which will weigh 3 ounces is MOST NEARLY

A. 250   B. 375   C. 450   D. 625

11. The sketch shown at the right shows the elevation of a part of a cone.
The length of the line XY is

A. 9"
B. 9 1/2"
C. 10"
D. 10 1/4"

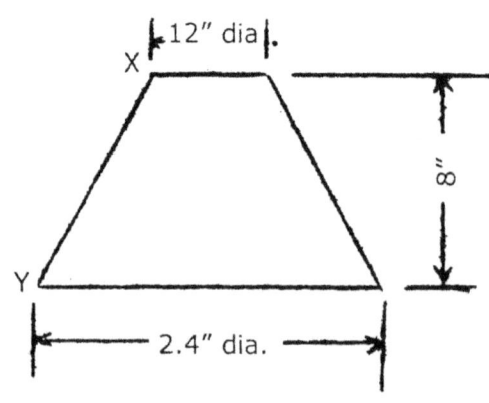

12. Two and two-thirds tees can be made from one sheet of steel. If 24 tees must be made, then the number of sheets required is MOST NEARLY

    A. 6   B. 7   C. 8   D. 9

13. Of the following materials, the BEST one to use as a tourniquet to stop bleeding from a severed artery is a(n)

    A. venetian blind cord   B. electric extension cord
    C. leather belt   D. shoelace

14. Of the following types of portable fire extinguishers, the one that should NOT be used to extinguish a fire around a blower motor is the _____ extinguisher.

    A. dry chemical   B. carbon dioxide
    C. liquefied gas   D. water solution

15. In setting a 16-foot extension ladder against a vertical wall, the SAFEST horizontal distance to set the foot of the ladder from the base of the wall is _____ ft.

    A. 2   B. 4   C. 6   D. 8

16. The sketch shown at the right represents a type of knot used in rigging. The knot is a

    A. clove hitch
    B. sheet bend
    C. square knot
    D. bowline

17. You are showing a new helper how to construct a complicated system of air ducts. Of the following, the helper is MOST likely to remember what you show him if you

    A. show him the entire job before permitting him to ask questions
    B. show him the hardest parts first, then go on to the easiest
    C. let him practice doing the things you show him
    D. show him both the right and the wrong ways to do it

18. Which of the following is the BEST way for you to make sure that your helper has understood a complicated instruction which you have given him?

    A. Ask the helper if he is sure that he has understood the instruction
    B. Ask the helper to repeat the instruction to you in his own words
    C. Watch the way the helper begins to follow the instruction
    D. Spot check the helper's progress in completing the instruction

Questions 19-20.

DIRECTIONS: Questions 19 and 20 are to be answered in accordance with the paragraph below.

    The cabinet shall be *fabricated* entirely of 22-gage stainless steel with #4 satin finish on all exposed surfaces. The face trim shall be one piece construction with no mitres or welding, 1" wide and 1/4" to the wall. All doors shall be mounted on heavy duty stainless steel piano hinges and have a concealed lock.

19. As used in the above paragraph, the word *fabricated* means MOST NEARLY   19.____

    A. made   B. designed   C. cut   D. plated

20. According to the above paragraph, a satin finish is to be used on surfaces   20.____

    A. to be welded
    B. that are visible
    C. on which the hinges are mounted
    D. that are to be covered

KEY (CORRECT ANSWERS)

1.	C	11.	C
2.	D	12.	D
3.	C	13.	C
4.	C	14.	D
5.	D	15.	B
6.	D	16.	D
7.	C	17.	C
8.	C	18.	B
9.	A	19.	A
10.	B	20.	B

EXAMINATION SECTION
TEST 1

DIRECTIONS: Each question or incomplete statement is followed by several suggested answers or completions. Select the one that BEST answers the question or completes the statement. *PRINT THE LETTER OF THE CORRECT ANSWER IN THE SPACE AT THE RIGHT.*

1. When sheet metal pipe with the seam on the inside is desired in order to have an unbroken outside surface, this will require a _____ seam. 1.____
   - A. countersunk grooved
   - B. folded
   - C. regular grooved
   - D. Pittsburgh

2. The process of forming sheet metal balls is called 2.____
   - A. mushrooming or malleting
   - B. raising or bumping
   - C. drawing or rounding
   - D. braking or blocking

3. If an uncoated 20-gauge metal sheet gauges 20 on a U.S. standard gauge, a 20-gauge galvanized metal sheet, when tested on the same gauge, will 3.____
   - A. actually gauge 18
   - B. actually gauge 19
   - C. also gauge 20
   - D. actually gauge 21

4. When the bottom of a large sheet metal container is to be joined to the body, it should be done by means of a _____ seam. 4.____
   - A. simple lap
   - B. grooved lock
   - C. common lock
   - D. double lock

5. The size designation of tinners' rivets is based on the 5.____
   - A. number of rivets per pound
   - B. rivet diameter only
   - C. weight per thousand rivets
   - D. length and diameter of the rivet

6. The decimal equivalent of 27/32 is MOST NEARLY 6.____
   - A. 0.813
   - B. 0.828
   - C. 0.844
   - D. 0.859

7. When a suitable machine is not available, sheet metal can be formed to a variety of shapes by the use of 7.____
   - A. bending slabs
   - B. flatters
   - C. bench stakes
   - D. swage blocks

8. If a riveted sheet metal seam is also soldered, this is MOST likely done in order to 8.____
   - A. strengthen the joint
   - B. provide a fillet for appearance
   - C. help set the rivets
   - D. make the seam watertight

9. When circular and semicircular bends must be made in sheet metal, it is necessary to use

   A. a *hold-down* attachment
   B. a cornice brake
   C. circular shears
   D. a setting-down machine

10. Small interior circles are MOST easily cut in sheet metal with _____ snips.

    A. straight
    B. combination
    C. bulldog
    D. hawksbill

11. When a pattern must be developed for a cylindrically-shaped intersected ventilation pipe to be used on a slanting roof, the method of development should be the _____ method.

    A. parallel line
    B. radial line
    C. angular
    D. triangular

12. In order to prevent thin sheet metal from buckling when riveting it to an angle iron, the BEST procedure to follow is to

    A. start riveting at one end of the sheet and work towards the other end
    B. start riveting at both ends of the sheet and work in towards the center
    C. install alternate rivets, working in one direction, and then fill in the remaining rivets working in the other direction
    D. start riveting in the center of the joint, working out in both directions

13. A man being instructed in the proper technique of cutting sheet metal with a hammer and chisel on a bench vise should be told that the BEST results will be obtained if he keeps his eye on the

    A. head of the hammer
    B. head of the chisel
    C. cutting edge of the chisel
    D. cutting line just ahead of the chisel

14. Of the following methods, the one that is NOT suitable for reinforcing the tops of sheet metal articles is

    A. hemming
    B. wiring
    C. riveting with band iron
    D. beveling

15. Condensation will MOST likely form on the inside surface of a skylight during _____ weather when the air inside the building is _____.

    A. cold; warm
    B. warm; warm
    C. cold; cold
    D. warm; cold

16. Two branch ventilating ducts, one 5 inches square and the other 12 inches square, are to connect to a square main duct. In order for the main duct to have the same cross-sectional area as the two branch ducts combined, the dimension of the main duct should be _____ inches square.

    A. 13
    B. 15
    C. 17
    D. 21

17. In sheet metal layout work, the flat steel square would MOST likely be used for constructing _____ from a base line.

    A. 45° and 90° angles
    B. angles other than 45° or 90°
    C. right angles and parallel lines
    D. right angles but not parallel lines

18. In order to form a rounded flange on the circular edge of a sheet metal cylinder so that it can receive a wire, it is necessary to use a _____ machine.

    A. wiring
    B. turning
    C. burring
    D. setting down

19. Rosin is used as the flux when soldering

    A. tin plate
    B. aluminum
    C. galvanized iron
    D. zinc

20. If the width of the lock called for in a grooved seam is 1/2", then the allowance to be added to each edge to be joined is

    A. 1/2"   B. 3/4"   C. 1"   D. 1 1/2"

KEY (CORRECT ANSWERS)

1.	A	11.	A
2.	B	12.	D
3.	B	13.	C
4.	D	14.	D
5.	C	15.	A
6.	C	16.	A
7.	C	17.	C
8.	D	18.	B
9.	B	19.	A
10.	D	20.	B

TEST 2

DIRECTIONS: Each question or incomplete statement is followed by several suggested answers or completions. Select the one that BEST answers the question or completes the statement. *PRINT THE LETTER OF THE CORRECT ANSWER IN THE SPACE AT THE RIGHT.*

1. Sheet metal of 0.025" thickness is to be riveted to a 1" x 1" x 1/8" angle iron, using 3/16" diameter rivets.
   If a length of rivet equal to 1 1/2 rivet diameters is needed to form a proper rivet head, then the rivets used for this job should have a shank length MOST NEARLY of

   A. 11/32"   B. 7/16"   C. 23/32"   D. 1 5/16"

   1._____

2. It is the function of a soldering flux to

   A. prevent the metals being soldered from overheating
   B. keep the soldering process from proceeding too rapidly for good metal fusion
   C. prevent oxidation from interfering with the soldering process
   D. keep the soldering process chemically neutral

   2._____

3. A 10" square ventilating duct is connected to a 5" square ventilating duct by a 20" long reducer. If air is flowing in the 10" duct at a speed of 1 foot per second, we can assume that it is flowing in the 5" duct at

   A. a faster speed
   B. a slower speed
   C. the same speed
   D. a faster or slower speed, depending on its temperature

   3._____

4. The distinction between sheet metal and metal plate is based upon _____ of material.

   A. type   B. flexibility
   C. thickness   D. density

   4._____

5. By comparison with the melting temperatures of the metals to be joined by soldering, the melting temperature of the solder used

   A. must be lower
   B. must be higher
   C. must be about the same
   D. may be either lower or higher, depending on which metals are being soldered

   5._____

6. When soldering the underside of a piece, it is normally good practice to tin and use only the working surface of the soldering copper instead of tinning all of its surfaces because, *otherwise,*

   A. the solder will be too hot for a good job
   B. the solder will have a tendency to flow away from the work
   C. the solder will be too cold for a good job
   D. too much solder will accumulate on the piece

   6._____

2 (#2)

7. A metal sheet 4'6" long is to have holes for spot welding drilled on a line parallel to the sheet. The holes are to be spaced 3 1/2" between centers, and the centers of the two end holes are to be 2 1/2" from the ends of the sheet. The number of holes to be drilled is

   A. 13 B. 14 C. 15 D. 16

8. If a scaled measurement of 1'3" on the drawing of a sheet metal layout represents an actual length of 10"0", then the drawing has been made to a scale of _____ inch to the foot.

   A. 3/4 B. 1 1/4 C. 1 1/2 D. 1 3/4

9. Light finishing work on the outside of a crowned sheet metal surface would usually be done with a _____ hammer.

   A. bumping B. machinist's
   C. dinging D. setting

10. A common flux for sheet metal is prepared by adding

    A. zinc to hydrochloric acid
    B. copper to sulfuric acid
    C. tin to nitric acid
    D. lead to acetic acid

11. When sheet metal is to be riveted, a rivet set is used to

    A. draw and upset the rivets but not head them
    B. upset and head the rivets but not draw them
    C. draw and head the rivets but not upset them
    D. draw, upset, and head the rivets

12. Assuming that it is desirable to have a minimum distance of at least 3 rivet diameters between centers of adjacent rivets and of at least 2 rivet diameters from the center of a rivet to the adjacent edge of a sheet, we could REASONABLY expect that an ordinary lap seam made with a single row of 5 rivets of 3/16" diameter would have a lap of _____ and a length of _____.

    A. 3/8"; 2 5/8"   B. 3/8"; 3"
    C. 3/4"; 2 5/8"   D. 3/4"; 3"

13. A tool that can be used both for scribing regular arcs and also transferring dimensions is the

    A. trammel   B. protractor
    C. scriber   D. combination square

14. The devices for clamping sheet metal in place on a squaring shear are the

    A. clamps   B. hold-downs
    C. guides   D. squares

15. When a hacksaw is used to cut sheet metal, the BEST blade to use is one with _____ teeth per inch.

    A. 14 B. 18 C. 24 D. 32

16. A tool which may be attached to a drill press and used to cut circles of 2 1/2 inch diameter or larger in sheet metal is the   16._____

    A. twist drill
    B. circular saw
    C. reamer
    D. hole saw

17. A versatile hand tool that can be used for a variety of sheet metalwork jobs such as bucking up rivet heads, straightening kinks in formed metal, forming seams, etc., is the   17._____

    A. hand dolly
    B. universal iron worker
    C. cupping tool
    D. set hammer

18. The gage of sheet metal is a measure of its   18._____

    A. thickness   B. area   C. length   D. width

19. A sheet metal plate has been cut in the form of a right triangle with sides of 5, 12, and 13 inches. The area of this plate is, in square inches,   19._____

    A. 30   B. 32 1/2   C. 60   D. 78

20. Of the following, the BEST reason for sheeting a sewer trench is to prevent   20._____

    A. the sewer from being covered with earth until after the final inspection
    B. water from seeping into the excavation
    C. the sides of the excavation from caving in during construction
    D. the sewer pipes being crushed

KEY (CORRECT ANSWERS)

1.	B	11.	C
2.	C	12.	D
3.	A	13.	A
4.	C	14.	B
5.	A	15.	D
6.	B	16.	D
7.	C	17.	A
8.	C	18.	A
9.	C	19.	A
10.	A	20.	C

EXAMINATION SECTION
TEST 1

DIRECTIONS: Each question or incomplete statement is followed by several suggested answers or completions. Select the one that BEST answers the question or completes the statement. *PRINT THE LETTER OF THE COREECT ANSWER IN THE SPACE AT THE RIGHT.*

Questions 1-4.

DIRECTIONS: Questions 1 through 4, inclusive, are based on the sketch of metal sheet shown below. (Sketch not to scale.)

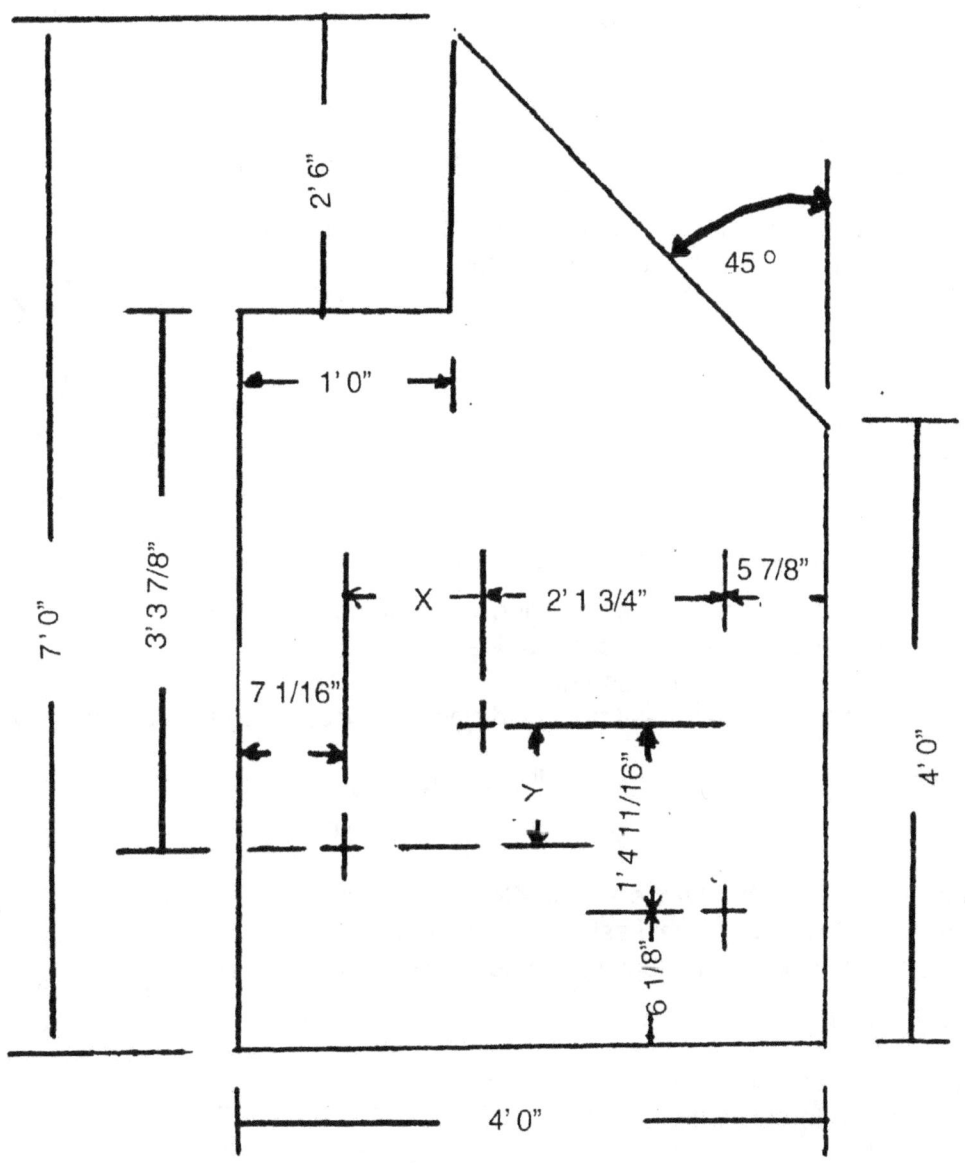

1. From the above sketch, the distance marked X is MOST NEARLY

   A. 5 1/4"   B. 6 5/16"   C. 7 1/8"   D. 9 5/16"

2. From the above sketch, the distance marked Y is MOST NEARLY

   A. 5 11/16"   B. 6 3/16"   C. 7 5/16"   D. 8 11/16"

3. In reference to the above sketch, if each piece is made from a rectangular piece of metal measuring 4' x 7', the percent of waste material is MOST NEARLY

   A. 10%   B. 15%   C. 25%   D. 30%

4. In reference to the above sketch, if the metal is 1/4" thick and weighs 144 pounds per cubic foot, the net weight of one piece would be MOST NEARLY _____ pounds.

   A. 51   B. 63   C. 75   D. 749

5. A *Pittsburgh lock* is a(n)

   A. emergency door lock   B. sheet metal joint
   C. elevator safety   D. boiler valve

6. If the shaded portion is cut from the plate shown, the area (in square inches) of the remaining portion is
   A. 26
   B. 29
   C. 32
   D. 58

7. Flux is used when soldering two pieces of sheet metal together in order to

   A. conduct the heat of the soldering iron to the sheets
   B. lower the melting point of the solder
   C. glue the solder to the sheets
   D. protect the sheet metal from oxidizing when heated by the soldering iron

8. Solder used for copper gutters is MOST frequently

   A. 30-70   B. 40-60   C. 50-50   D. 60-40

9. Specifications for hollow metal doors to be used on a construction state: Double door without mullions. Spot weld astragal to inactive door.
   Astragal, as used in the above statement, means MOST NEARLY

   A. louver   B. hinge   C. molding   D. veneer

10. The width, in inches, of each of the identical slots in the plate is
    A. 1/4
    B. 3/16
    C. 1/8
    D. 1/16

11. Metal gutters are MOST commonly made of

   A. stainless steel B. copper
   C. monel metal D. brass

12. The type of seam GENERALLY used in the construction of sheet metal cylinders of small diameters is the _____ seam.

   A. double-edged B. folded
   C. double-hemmed D. simple lap

13. With respect to soldering, it is LEAST important that

   A. the soldering copper be clean and well-tinned
   B. a good flux suitable for the metal being soldered be used
   C. the joint to be soldered be well-cleaned
   D. a lot of solder be used

14. When two sheet metal plates are riveted together, a specified minimum distance must be provided from the edge of each plate to the nearest line of rivets in order to prevent

   A. the rivet heads from working loose
   B. the rivets from being sheared
   C. tearing of the material between the rivets and the edges of the plates
   D. excessive stress on the rivets

15. It is BEST to cut a piece of sheet metal with a pair of snips by starting each cut with the metal sheet

   A. out near the points of the snips
   B. as far back in the jaws as possible
   C. midway between the snip points and the pivot
   D. one-quarter the way between the snip points and the pivot

16. A sheet metal plate has been cut in the form of a right triangle with sides of 5, 12, and 13 inches.
    The area of this plate, in square inches, is

   A. 30 B. 32 1/2 C. 60 D. 78

17. To form the head of a tinner's rivet, the PROPER tool to use is a rivet

   A. anvil B. plate C. set D. brake

18. The area of the metal plate shown at the right, minus the hole area, is MOST NEARLY _____ square inches.

   A. 8.5
   B. 8.9
   C. 9.4
   D. 10.1

19.

The center punch is numbered

A. 1　　　　B. 2　　　　C. 3　　　　D. 4

20. Leather gloves should be worn when handling sheet metal PRIMARILY because

   A. pressure on the metal might cause it to bend
   B. the edges and corners of the metal may be sharp
   C. natural oil or moisture from hands corrodes the metal
   D. leather provides a more secure grip

21. A type of rivet which can be put in place even when a worker does NOT have access to the back side of the work is known as a _____ rivet.

   A. bucking　　　　B. double-head
   C. pop　　　　　　D. side

22. The open-top tin box shown at the right can be made by bending along the dotted lines of the flat cut sheet marked

   A.　　　　B.　　　　C.　　　　D.

23. The BEST flux to use when soldering galvanized iron is

   A. killed acid　　　　B. sal-ammoniac
   C. muriatic acid　　　D. resin

24. When soldering a vertical joint, the soldering iron should be tinned on _____ side(s).

   A. one　　　　B. two　　　　C. three　　　　D. four

25. The thickness of a sheet of 16-ounce copper is MOST NEARLY _____ inch.

   A. 1/50　　　　B. 1/30　　　　C. 1/20　　　　D. 1/8

KEY (CORRECT ANSWERS)

1. D
2. D
3. C
4. B
5. B

6. C
7. D
8. C
9. C
10. C

11. B
12. D
13. D
14. C
15. B

16. A
17. C
18. B
19. A
20. B

21. C
22. D
23. C
24. A
25. A

TEST 2

DIRECTIONS: Each question or incomplete statement is followed by several suggested answers or completions. Select the one that BEST answers the question or completes the statement. *PRINT THE LETTER OF THE CORRECT ANSWER IN THE SPACE AT THE RIGHT.*

1. When drilling a small hole in sheet copper, the BEST practice is to

   A. make a dent with a center punch first
   B. put some cutting oil at the point you intend to drill
   C. use a slow speed drill to prevent overheating
   D. use an auger type bit

   1.____

2. The reason for annealing sheet copper is to make it

   A. soft and easier to work
   B. more resistant to weather
   C. easier to solder
   D. harder and more resistant to blows

   2.____

3. In draw filing,

   A. only the edge of the file is used
   B. a triangle file is generally used
   C. the file is pulled toward the mechanic's body in filing
   D. the file must have a safe edge

   3.____

4. The dimension X on the plate is
   A. 1 7/8"
   B. 2 1/8"
   C. 2 1/4"
   D. 2 3/8"

   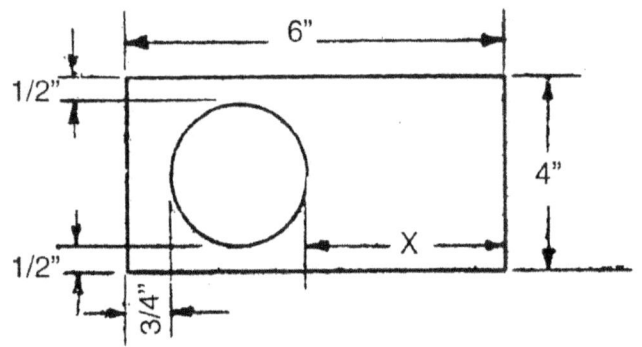

   4.____

5. One advantage of using a Pittsburgh lock seam when joining two pieces of sheet metal is that, once formed in the shop, it may be assembled anywhere with a

   A. hickey   B. swage   C. template   D. mallet

   5.____

6. White cast iron is

   A. hard and brittle   B. hard and ductile
   C. ductile and malleable   D. brittle and malleable

   6.____

7. The gage used for measuring copper wire is

   A. U.S. Standard   B. Stubbs
   C. Washburn and Moen   D. Brown and Sharpe

   7.____

52

8. The difference between *right hand* and *left hand* tin snips is the

   A. relative position of the cutting jaws
   B. shape of the cutting jaws
   C. shape of the handles
   D. relative position of the handles

9. A machine used to bend sheet metal is called a

   A. router   B. planer   C. brake   D. swage

10. The type of solder that would be used in *hard soldering* would be _____ solder.

    A. bismuth   B. wiping   C. 50-50   D. silver

11. The MAXIMUM number of 2 inch by 3 inch rectangular pieces which can be cut from the metal sheet is
    A. 8
    B. 6
    C. 4
    D. 2

    METAL SHEET — 5 1/4" × 8 1/4"

12. The thin sheet piece when properly folded will form a closed box with a square top and bottom.
    Dimension Z of the box will be
    A. 2
    B. 4
    C. 6
    D. 8

    THIN SHEET PIECE — 16"; BOX — 10", Z

13. Sheet metal seams are sometimes grooved. The MAIN function of the grooving is to

    A. facilitate making a soldered joint
    B. prevent unlocking
    C. improve the appearance of the joint
    D. save sheet metal

14. The area, in square inches, of the plate shown at the right is
    A. 32
    B. 52
    C. 58
    D. 64

15. Shown at the right is an open-top round tin container. In order to make the container so that the metal used for the bottom area (πR^2) is equal to the metal used for the cylindrical side area ($2\pi Rh$), the radius R must be equal to
    A. 1/2"
    B. 1"
    C. 2"
    D. 4"

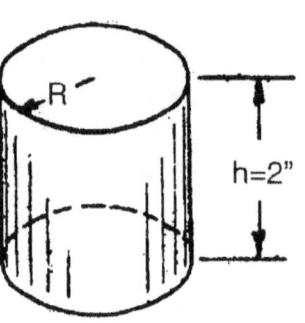

15.____

16. On a drawing, the following standard cross-section represents MOST NEARLY
    A. malleable iron
    B. steel
    C. bronze
    D. lead

16.____

17. On the curved metal sheet, the distance X is, in inches,
    A. 3
    B. 4
    C. 5
    D. 6

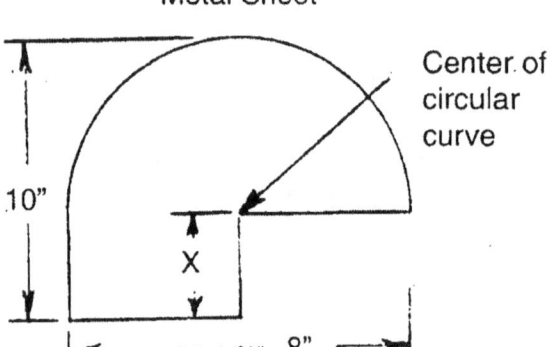

17.____

18. If the piece of sheet metal is to be cylindrically formed into a hand scoop by soldering edges X and Y together, then the resultant scoop will be No.
    A. 1
    B. 2
    C. 3
    D. 4

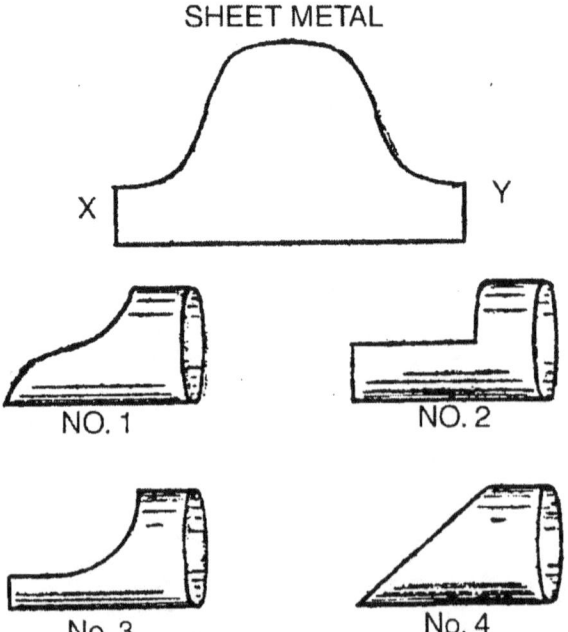

18.____

54

19. Copper sheet is USUALLY specified in   19._____

    A. Birmingham gage
    B. ounces per square foot
    C. ounces per square yard
    D. pounds per square yard

20. The United States Standard Gage is used to measure sheet metal thicknesses of   20._____

    A. tin
    B. aluminum
    C. bronze
    D. iron and steel

KEY (CORRECT ANSWERS)

1.	A	11.	B
2.	A	12.	B
3.	C	13.	B
4.	C	14.	C
5.	D	15.	D
6.	A	16.	C
7.	D	17.	D
8.	A	18.	A
9.	C	19.	C
10.	D	20.	D

EXAMINATION SECTION
TEST 1

DIRECTIONS: Each question or incomplete statement is followed by several suggested answers or completions. Select the one that BEST answers the question or completes the statement. *PRINT THE LETTER OF THE CORRECT ANSWER IN TE SPACE AT THE RIGHT.*

1. The hole size for a 1/2"-13" NC tapped hole maintaining a 65% thread height is   1._____
   A. 25/64"   B. 7/16"   C. 31/64"   D. 33/64"

2. A good flux for black iron is   2._____
   A. zinc chloride   B. rosin
   C. resin   D. sal ammoniac

3. The unified thread system which provides for an interchange of parts manufactured in   3._____
   the United States, Great Britain, and Canada is a combination of the _____ thread and
   the _____ thread.
   A. American national form; whitworth
   B. sharp V; acme
   C. American national form; acme
   D. American national form; sellers

4. The pan head of self-tapping screw, with a gimlet point, used for fastening light sheet   4._____
   metal, is referred to as type
   A. A   B. B   C. C   D. D

5. Terne plate is black iron coated with a mixture of   5._____
   A. lead and tin   B. lead and zinc
   C. lead and nickel   D. tin and zinc

6. The worm gear of a thread chasing dial is designed to mesh with the   6._____
   A. feed screw   B. split nut
   C. lead screw   D. gear rack

7. The taper per foot for an American standard taper pin is   7._____
   A. 1/16"   B. 1/8"   C. 3/32"   D. 1/4"

8. To give a cutting speed of 35 f.p.m., a 3/4" drill should be run at about _____ r.p.m.   8._____
   A. 70   B. 176   C. 280   D. 350

9. The kaws on a pair of combination snips are   9._____
   A. curved   B. serrated   C. notched   D. straight

10. The taper that MOST closely resembles the Morse taper is known as the   10._____
    A. Pratt and Whitney   B. Sellers
    C. Jarno   D. Brown and Sharpe

57

11. The gage used to set the threading tool in the lathe is called a(n) _____ gage.

    A. center   B. thread   C. pitch   D. angle

12. Ten-point steel has a carbon content of

    A. .010%   B. .10%   C. 1%   D. 10%

13. The conductor stake used in sheet metal work has

    A. a round, slender horn and a rectangular horn
    B. two tapered horns of different diameters
    C. one slender horn and two shanks
    D. two cylindrical horns of different diameters

14. When draw filing a piece of cold rolled steel 1/2" x 1/2" x 6", the BEST file to use is the

    A. vixon   B. XF
    C. mill   D. double cut smooth

15. Babbitt is an alloy of copper, tin, and

    A. antimony   B. zinc   C. aluminum   D. nickel

16. The hand reamer that lends itself BEST to reaming a pulley hole with a keyway is the _____ reamer.

    A. adjustable hand   B. straight tooth
    C. spiral tooth   D. increment cut

17. An acme thread has an included angle of

    A. 29°   B. 55°   C. 59 1/2°   D. 60°

18. The straight single depth of a 1/2"-13 American national form thread is

    A. .0375   B. .0423   C. .0499   D. .0562

19. A four inch cylinder made of 1 X tin, joined with a #4 grooved seam, should have a stock allowance for the seam equal to

    A. 2 1/2 times the width of the seam plus 4 times the thickness of the metal
    B. 3 times the width of the seam
    C. 3 1/2 times the width of the seam plus twice the thickness of the metal
    D. 3 times the width of the seam plus three times the thickness of the metal

20. The process of heating cold rolled steel, impregnating with a carbonaceous material, and quenching is known as

    A. normalizing   B. nitriding
    C. case-hardening   D. spherodizing

21. A solder made of 60% tin and 40% lead melts at _____°F.

    A. 370   B. 415   C. 430   D. 461

22. A steel or wrought-iron block, other than the anvil, that is used for forge work is the _____ block.

    A. forming   B. vee   C. shaping   D. swage

23. A gate for a mold should always be shaped so that it

    A. is parallel to the drag surface
    B. slopes toward the mold
    C. slopes away from the mold
    D. connects with the heavy section of the pattern

24. Graphite is sometimes used in foundry practice as a

    A. binder for the sand
    B. binder for small cores
    C. mold facing
    D. material for making gaggers and chaplets

25. A newly developed structural steel that puts weather to work to protect itself and requires no painting is known as

    A. Stan-Steel   B. Ketos
    C. Cor-Ten   D. Armco

26. The process of heating and quenching tool steel from a temperature either within or above the critical temperature range is known as

    A. annealing   B. tempering
    C. hardening   D. normalizing

27. Of the following, the information that is NOT part of the manufacturer's grinding wheel marking symbols is

    A. grain size   B. grade
    C. wheel shape   D. structure

28. The rapid dulling of a twist drill, especially at the outer end of the lips (corners), is evidence that the

    A. drill has excessive lip clearance
    B. drill is revolving too rapidly
    C. point has been ground to an angle of less than 118°
    D. drill is riding on its *heel*

29. The size of a lathe mandrel or arbor is designated

    A. on the small end
    B. in accordance with standards set by individual manufacturers
    C. on the large end
    D. on both ends

30. The numbered lines on the barrel of a micrometer are in increments of 30._____
    A. .001"   B. .005"   C. .025"   D. .100"

KEY (CORRECT ANSWERS)

1. B   16. C
2. A   17. A
3. A   18. C
4. A   19. B
5. A   20. C

6. C   21. A
7. D   22. D
8. B   23. C
9. D   24. C
10. C   25. C

11. A   26. C
12. B   27. C
13. D   28. B
14. C   29. C
15. A   30. D

TEST 2

DIRECTIONS: Each question or incomplete statement is followed by several suggested answers or completions. Select the one that BEST answers the question or completes the statement. *PRINT THE LETTER OF THE CORRECT ANSWER IN THE SPACE AT THE RIGHT.*

1. To tap a hole for 1/8" standard pipe, one should use a tap designated 1/8 -   1.____
   A. 13 NSP   B. 20 NPT   C. 23 NTP   D. 27 NPT

2. A promising development in steel technology to produce BETTER steel more efficiently is   2.____
   A. modern blooming   B. continuous casting
   C. wet rolling   D. rapid ingot teaming

3. The spindle bore of an engine lathe is USUALLY equipped with a _____ taper.   3.____
   A. Morse   B. Brown and Sharpe
   C. Pratt and Whitney   D. Sellers

4. The space from the edge of the metal to the center of the rivet line should be AT LEAST _____ times the diameter of the rivet.   4.____
   A. 1 1/2   B. 2   C. 3   D. 4

5. A good forging heat for steel is   5.____
   A. cherry red (1375° F)   B. blood red (1075° F)
   C. light yellow (1975° F)   D. white (2200° F)

6. The tools BEST suited to forge a shoulder are the _____ and sledge.   6.____
   A. top fuller   B. bottom fuller
   C. set hammer   D. hardie

7. A base box is the unit of measure for tin plate and contains _____ sheets _____.   7.____
   A. 56; 18" x 20"   B. 100; 20" x 28"
   C. 112; 14" x 20"   D. 128; 18" x 20"

8. Of the following, the stake BEST suited for forming a common funnel is the   8.____
   A. creasing   B. blow horn
   C. beakhorn   D. candlemold

9. The body of sand used to form a recess or opening in a casting is called a   9.____
   A. core   B. core print
   C. fillet   D. cored hole

10. Tin plate with a light coating of tin is called _____ plate.   10.____
    A. coke tin   B. charcoal tin
    C. dairy   D. terne

11. The gage used to measure the thickness of iron and steel sheet metal is

    A. American
    B. United States standard
    C. Brown and Sharpe
    D. stubs

12. If a cross-feed screw on a lathe has eight threads per inch, and the micrometer dial is graduated so that a single division indicates a movement of one one-thousandth of an inch, the micrometer dial will have _____ equal divisions.

    A. 90   B. 100   C. 125   D. 250

13. Screws for use in metal, whose size is designated by a gage number indicating the diameter of the body of the screw, are called

    A. set screws
    B. machine bolts
    C. cap screws
    D. machine screws

14. An accurate method of checking the size of a twist drill would be to use a micrometer to measure the

    A. body of the drill
    B. point of the drill across the land
    C. point of the drill across the margin
    D. flute of the drill

15. If the cutting speed of steel is 75 feet per minute when using a high speed steel cutter to turn a 1 1/2" diameter piece of steel, the spindle speed of the lathe should be _____ RPM.

    A. 75   B. 186   C. 200   D. 340

16. In foundry, the process of making a mold in sand from a pattern with an irregular parting line USUALLY involves

    A. coping down
    B. a lost wax process
    C. a split pattern
    D. a sweep mold

17. The cutting action of a twist drill is aided by a *rake* action which is provided for on the drill by the

    A. web   B. flute   C. land   D. margin

18. The included angle on the head of a standard flat-head machine screw is

    A. 60°   B. 90°   C. 82°   D. 59°

19. The main alloying elements in monel metal are

    A. nickel, zinc, copper
    B. chrome, nickel, copper
    C. copper, zinc, tin
    D. nickel, copper

20. When turning a slender rod in a lathe, springing is minimized by using a

    A. compound rest
    B. follower rest
    C. cross rest
    D. draw-in bar

21. In foundry practice, a strike bar is used for 21._____

    A. loosening the pattern
    B. striking off flashing
    C. separating cope and drag
    D. making sand even with top of flask

22. The forge operation of enlarging the cross-sectional area of a bar is called 22._____

    A. upsetting   B. drawing out
    C. fullering   D. spreading

23. A screw thread that is NOT used much today is the 23._____

    A. acme   B. square
    C. American standard D. S.A.E.

24. One of the first men to produce carbide tools was 24._____

    A. Johannson   B. Metcalf   C. Jarno   D. Moissan

25. The twist drill that is exactly the same diameter as the letter *E* drill is 25._____

    A. 1/4"   B. #40   C. #1   D. 5/16"

26. The cross-sectional shape of a warding file is 26._____

    A. square
    B. tapered wedge
    C. rectangular (wide and thin)
    D. rectangular (wide and thick)

27. The steel that would lend itself BEST for making a center punch is 27._____

    A. high speed   B. 1020 machinery
    C. cold rolled   D. drill rod

28. One thousand 10 oz. rivets weigh about 28._____

    A. 1000 x 10 oz.   B. 10 oz.
    C. 1 lb.   D. 10 lbs.

29. A good flux for tin plate is 29._____

    A. zinc chloride   B. muriatic acid
    C. rosin   D. cut acid

30. The material that gives high-speed steel its hardness and ability to keep an edge is 30._____

    A. tungsten   B. vanadium   C. chromium   D. platinum

KEY (CORRECT ANSWERS)

1.	D	16.	A
2.	B	17.	B
3.	A	18.	C
4.	B	19.	D
5.	C	20.	B
6.	C	21.	D
7.	C	22.	A
8.	B	23.	B
9.	A	24.	D
10.	A	25.	A
11.	B	26.	C
12.	C	27.	D
13.	D	28.	B
14.	C	29.	C
15.	C	30.	B

TEST 3

DIRECTIONS: Each question or incomplete statement is followed by several suggested answers or completions. Select the one that BEST answers the question or completes the statement. *PRINT THE LETTER OF THE CORRECT ANSWER IN THE SPACE AT THE RIGHT.*

1. A metal that has a coating of zinc is known as a(n) _____ metal. 1.____
   - A. nitrided
   - B. anodized
   - C. galvanized
   - D. normalized

2. A set of hand taps includes _____ taps. 2.____
   - A. machine, plug, and bottom
   - B. taper, plug, and machine
   - C. taper, machine, and bottom
   - D. taper, plug, and bottom

3. The pitch of the threads in a micrometer sleeve is _____ threads per inch. 3.____
   - A. 25   B. 40   C. 100   D. 1,000

4. The motion of the shaper ram is. 4.____
   - A. circular
   - B. rotary
   - C. reciprocating
   - D. semi-circular

5. A split die 5.____
   - A. is damaged beyond repair
   - B. can be adjusted
   - C. requires two wrenches to operate
   - D. contains two separate cutters

6. The diameter of a twist drill is measured across the 6.____
   - A. margin   B. web   C. flutes   D. shank

7. A template is a 7.____
   - A. type of hand shears
   - B. metal cutting saw
   - C. pattern
   - D. type of pin punch

8. The tool post is mounted in the clapper box in a 8.____
   - A. lathe
   - B. drill press
   - C. milling machine
   - D. shaper

9. To remove a taper shank drill from a drill press, use a 9.____
   - A. drift punch
   - B. pin punch
   - C. pipe wrench
   - D. chuck key

10. One complete turn of the handle on the index head of a milling machine will turn the work 10.____
    - A. 180°   B. 9°   C. 40°   D. 90°

65

11. Offsetting the tailstock on the lathe will   11._____

    A. facilitate boring
    B. enable threads to be cut accurately
    C. center-drill without oil
    D. produce a taper

12. A rack and pinion on a lathe give movement to the   12._____

    A. carriage   B. tailstock
    C. headstock   D. compound rest

13. A knurling tool is used in a   13._____

    A. milling machine   B. shaper
    C. lathe   D. drill press

14. The dead center in a lathe is found in the   14._____

    A. headstock   B. compound rest
    C. cross slide   D. tailstock

15. Lathe tool bits are made of _____ steel.   15._____

    A. low carbon   B. high speed
    C. machine   D. case hardened

16. The products of the blast furnace are   16._____

    A. waste gases, steel, and slag
    B. coke, slag, and pig iron
    C. waste gases, pig iron, and slag
    D. waste gases, coke, and slag

17. Solder is composed of _____ and lead.   17._____

    A. zinc   B. tin   C. copper   D. spelter

18. On a double thread, the lead is equal to   18._____

    A. the pitch   B. one-half the pitch
    C. twice the pitch   D. diameter

19. A vernier scale can be found on a   19._____

    A. height gage   B. surface plate
    C. dial indicator   D. telescope gage

20. The lines on the sleeve of a micrometer are _____ of an inch apart.   20._____

    A. .075   B. .025   C. .100   D. .001

21. An Allen head screw is tightened with a   21._____

    A. regular screwdriver
    B. spanner wrench
    C. cross-shaped screwdriver
    D. hexagon-shaped wrench

22. The handle of a file fits on the

    A. tang B. heel C. tail D. sole

23. Countersinks for flat head screws have an included angle of

    A. 60° B. 75° C. 82° D. 90°

24. A hand groover is used to

    A. remove chips from a groove or keyway
    B. lock a seam
    C. fold over a wired edge
    D. shape soft metal on a lathe

25. An example of a ferrous metal is

    A. brass B. aluminum C. iron D. copper

26. The cold chisel commonly used to shape a keyway is a

    A. cape chisel B. flat chisel
    C. round chisel D. diamond point

27. A foundry flask is used to

    A. analyze the sand B. clean the pattern
    C. support the sand D. clean the casting

28. A sprue pin is used to

    A. ram a pattern
    B. provide a hole through which the metal is poured
    C. locate the two halves of a split pattern
    D. clean the slag off molten metal

29. The sand used to separate the cope from the drag is _____ sand.

    A. parting B. green C. core D. tempered

30. Fillets are used to

    A. simplify construction of the mold
    B. strengthen the casting
    C. strengthen the pattern
    D. support sand cores

KEY (CORRECT ANSWERS)

1. C
2. D
3. B
4. C
5. B

6. A
7. C
8. D
9. A
10. B

11. D
12. A
13. C
14. D
15. B

16. C
17. B
18. C
19. A
20. B

21. D
22. A
23. C
24. B
25. C

26. A
27. C
28. B
29. A
30. B

TEST 4

DIRECTIONS: Each question or incomplete statement is followed by several suggested answers or completions. Select the one that BEST answers the question or completes the statement. *PRINT THE LETTER OF THE CORRECT ANSWER IN THE SPACE AT THE RIGHT.*

1. The suggested cutting speed for high-speed drills when drilling steel is APPROXIMATELY _____ surface feet per minute.   1._____

   A.   200-250   B.   150-200   C.   100-150   D.   50-100

2. When a strong joint is needed to connect the bottom of a sheet-metal container to the body, the BEST joint to use is a   2._____

   A.   burr or flange   B.   single seam
   C.   double seam   D.   dovetail seam

3. The candle-mould stake   3._____

   A.   is used for shaping sheet-metal candlestick holders
   B.   has a slender horn for tube forming
   C.   is used mainly for corner seam closing
   D.   is used for wiring and beading

4. Left-hand aviation snips are designed to   4._____

   A.   cut a curve to the left
   B.   be used by left-handed people
   C.   cut a curve to the right
   D.   cut aluminum airplane parts

5. Ammonium chloride is also known as   5._____

   A.   sal ammoniac
   B.   bauxite
   C.   amino acid
   D.   a good electro-plating electrolyte

6. As the percentage of lead in soft solder increases, the   6._____

   A.   melting point becomes higher
   B.   melting point becomes lower
   C.   strength of the joint decreases
   D.   percentage of zinc decreases

7. To improve the machinability and resistance to corrosion of aluminum, the alloying metal is   7._____

   A.   silicon   B.   copper   C.   manganese   D.   magnesium

8. Borax can be used   8._____

   A.   as a flux in brazing
   B.   for pickling silver

69

C. as an adhesive in copper enameling
D. as a cutting compound

9. A 42-tooth driving gear rotating at 400 RPM in a clockwise direction is connected to a 14-tooth gear by means of an idler gear.
   The speed and direction of rotation of the (14-tooth) driven gear is

   A. 1200 RPM and rotating clockwise
   B. 1200 RPM and rotating counter-clockwise
   C. 133 1/3 RPM and rotating counter-clockwise
   D. 133 1/3 RPM and rotating clockwise

10. Rouge used in metal polishing is made of

    A. decomposed shale   B. iron oxide
    C. powdered lava   D. silicon carbide

11. The BEST thickness of copper for doing repousse projects is _____ gauge.

    A. 14   B. 18   C. 24   D. 36

12. Copper is often pickled with

    A. a solution of sulphuric acid and water
    B. a solution of ammonium sulphide
    C. powdered tragacenth and alcohol
    D. kasenit

13. Liver of sulphur is also known as

    A. ferric sulphide   B. hyposulphite of soda
    C. potassium sulphide   D. sulphur dioxide

14. *German Silver* is USUALLY made of about

    A. 92% tin, 6% antimony, and 2% copper
    B. 64% copper, 18% nickel, and 18% zinc
    C. 925 parts of silver and 75 parts of copper
    D. 85% copper and 15% zinc

15. Blowholes in castings can be avoided by the use of

    A. a gate   B. vents
    C. a sprue pin   D. a core print

16. Chaplets are used

    A. with match-plate patterns
    B. to support cores
    C. in investment casting
    D. in shell mold casting

17. Muriatic acid is the same as

    A. hydrochloric acid   B. nitric acid
    C. sulphuric acid   D. aqua regia

18. Most of the steel made today is made in a(n).

    A. open-hearth furnace B. Bessemer converter
    C. electric furnace D. blast furnace

19. Nitriding is a process used for hardening

    A. special steel alloys by using ammonia gas
    B. low carbon steels
    C. steel parts requiring shallow surface hardness
    D. steel by exposing it while heated to a carbonaceous material

20. An aluminum oxide abrasive wheel is intended especially for grinding

    A. brass B. iron C. aluminum D. steel

21. A scleroscope is used to

    A. examine crystalline structure
    B. determine hardness
    C. measure with extreme accuracy
    D. identify metal

22. The United States Standard (USS) gauge is used for measuring

    A. drills from #1 to #80
    B. steel wire, sheets, and plates
    C. copper, brass, and aluminum
    D. machine screw sizes #0 to #12

23. Back gears are USUALLY used on a lathe when

    A. knurling
    B. boring a hole
    C. reversing the feed
    D. high spindle speed is needed

24. The axes of spur gears are aligned so that they GENERALLY

    A. intersect at right angles
    B. intersect at acute angles
    C. intersect at obtuse angles
    D. are parallel to each other

25. The BEST file for filing steel on the lathe is a _____ file.

    A. vixen
    B. double-cut warding
    C. second-cut pillar
    D. long angle single-cut mill

26. In lathe work, the formula to use to determine the correct spindle speed when V = cutting speed in feet per minute, and D = diameter of workpiece in inches, is:

    A. $RPM = \dfrac{12\pi}{VD}$ B. $RPM = \dfrac{12V}{\pi D}$ C. $RPM = \dfrac{\pi D}{12V}$ D. $RPM = \dfrac{\pi V}{12D}$

27. The CORRECT sequence of drill sizes from smallest to largest is: 27._____

    A. #60, #30, 7/32", M
    B. #7, #50, 1/4", F
    C. #14, #2, Q, 1/8"
    D. B, R, 3/8", #12

28. The taper per foot on a part 2 5/16" in length and with a 15/16" diameter at one end and 11/16" at the other end, is 28._____

    A. .578"   B. .770"   C. .925"   D. 1.297"

29. The MAJOR diameter of a 5-40 NC machine screw is 29._____

    A. .125"   B. .140"   C. .155"   D. .170"

30. The usual amount left for removal with a reamer is 30._____

    A. 1/8" to 1/16"
    B. 1/16" to 1/32"
    C. 1/32" to 1/64"
    D. 1/64" to .005"

KEY (CORRECT ANSWERS)

1.	D	16.	B
2.	C	17.	A
3.	B	18.	A
4.	C	19.	A
5.	A	20.	D
6.	A	21.	B
7.	D	22.	B
8.	A	23.	A
9.	A	24.	A
10.	B	25.	D
11.	D	26.	B
12.	A	27.	A
13.	C	28.	D
14.	B	29.	A
15.	B	30.	D

ARITHMETICAL REASONING
EXAMINATION SECTION
TEST 1

DIRECTIONS: Each question or incomplete statement is followed by several suggested answers or completions. Select the one that BEST answers the question or completes the statement. *PRINT THE LETTER OF THE CORRECT ANSWER IN THE SPACE AT THE RIGHT.*

1. A supplier quotes a list price of $172.00 less 15 and 10 percent for twelve tools. The actual cost for these twelve tools is MOST NEARLY   1.____

   A. $146   B. $132   C. $129   D. $112

2. If the diameter of a circular piece of sheet metal is 1 1/2 feet, the area, in square inches, is MOST NEARLY   2.____

   A. 1.77   B. 2.36   C. 254   D. 324

3. The sum of 5'6", 7'3", 9'3 1/2", and 3'7 1/4" is   3.____

   A. 19'8 1/2"   B. 22' 1/2"   C. 25'7 3/4"   D. 28'8 3/4"

4. If the floor area of one shop is 15' by 21'3" and the size of an adjacent shop is 18' by 30'6", then the TOTAL floor area of these two shops is _____ square feet.   4.____

   A. 1127.75   B. 867.75   C. 549.0   D. 318.75

5. The fraction which is equal to 0.875 is   5.____

   A. 7/16   B. 5/8   C. 3/4   D. 7/8

6. The sum of 1/2, 2 1/32, 4 3/16, and 1 7/8 is MOST NEARLY   6.____

   A. 9.593   B. 9.625   C. 9.687   D. 10.593

7. If the base of a right triangle is 9" and the altitude is 12", the length of the third side will be   7.____

   A. 13"   B. 14"   C. 15"   D. 16"

8. If a steel bar 1" in diameter and 12' long weighs 32 lbs., then the weight of a piece of this bar 5'9" long is MOST NEARLY _____ lbs.   8.____

   A. 15.33   B. 15.26   C. 16.33   D. 15.06

9. The diameter of a circle whose circumference is 12" is MOST NEARLY   9.____

   A. 3.82"   B. 3.72"   C. 3.62"   D. 3.52"

10. A dimension of 39/64 inches converted to decimals is MOST NEARLY   10.____

    A. .600"   B. .609"   C. .607"   D. .611"

11. A farm worker was paid a weekly wage of $415.20 for a 44-hour work week. As a result of a new labor contract, he is paid $431.40 a week for a 40-hour work week with time and one-half pay for time worked in excess of 40 hours in any work week.
If he continues to work 44 hours weekly under the new contract, the amount by which his average hourly rate for a 44-hour work week under the new contract exceeds the hourly rate previously paid him lies between _____ and _____, inclusive.

    A. 80¢; $1.00
    B. $1.00; $1.20
    C. $1.25; $1.45
    D. $1.50; $1.70

11._____

12. The sum of 4 feet 3 1/4 inches, 7 feet 2 1/2 inches, and 11 feet 1/4 inch is _____ feet _____ inches.

    A. 21; 6 1/4
    B. 22; 6
    C. 23; 5
    D. 24; 5 3/4

12._____

13. The number 0.038 is read as

    A. 38 tenths
    B. 38 hundredths
    C. 38 thousandths
    D. 38 ten-thousandths

13._____

14. Assume that an employee is paid at the rate of $10.86 per hour with time and a half for overtime past 40 hours in a week.
If he works 43 hours in a week, his gross weekly pay is

    A. $434.40
    B. $438.40
    C. $459.18
    D. $483.27

14._____

15. The sum of the following dimensions: 3'2 1/4", 8 7/8", 2'6 3/8", 2'9 3/4", and 1'0" is

    A. 16'7 1/4"
    B. 10'7 1/4"
    C. 10'3 1/4"
    D. 9'3 1/4"

15._____

16. Two gears are meshed together and have a gear ratio of 6 to 1.
If the small gear rotates 120 revolutions per minute, the large gear rotates at

    A. 20
    B. 40
    C. 60
    D. 720

16._____

17. The vacuum side of a compound gage reads 14 inches of vacuum. The barometer reading is 29.76 inches of mercury. The equivalent absolute pressure of the compound gage reading, in inches of mercury, is MOST likely

    A. 15.06
    B. 15.76
    C. 43.06
    D. 43.76

17._____

18. The fraction 5/8 expressed as a decimal is

    A. 0.125
    B. 0.412
    C. 0.625
    D. 0.875

18._____

19. If 300 feet of a certain size pipe weighs 450 pounds, the number of pounds that 100 feet will weigh is

    A. 1,350
    B. 150
    C. 300
    D. 250

19._____

20. As an oiler, you work for a facility that has automobiles that use, on the average, 600 quarts of one grade of lubricating oil every month.
The number of one-gallon cans of the above oil that should be ordered each month to meet this requirement is

    A. 100
    B. 125
    C. 140
    D. 150

20._____

21. The inside dimensions of a rectangular oil gravity tank are: height 15", width 9", length 10".
    The amount of oil in the tank, in gallons, (231 cu.in. = 1 gallon), when the oil level is 9" high, is MOST NEARLY

    A. 2.3   B. 3.5   C. 5.2   D. 5.8

22. If 30 gallons of oil cost $76.80, 45 gallons of oil at the same rate will cost

    A. $91.20   B. $115.20   C. $123.20   D. $131.20

23. If an oiler earns $18,000 in the first six months of a year and receives a 10% raise in salary for the next six months of the same year, his TOTAL earnings for the year will be

    A. $36,000   B. $37,500   C. $37,800   D. $39,600

24. If the cost of lubricating oil increases 15%, then a gallon of oil which used to cost $10.00 will now cost MOST NEARLY

    A. $10.50   B. $11.00   C. $11.50   D. $12.00

25. The sum of 7/8", 3/4", 1/2", and 3/8" is

    A. 2 1/8"   B. 2 1/4"   C. 2 3/8"   D. 2 1/2"

KEY (CORRECT ANSWERS)

1. B
2. C
3. C
4. B
5. D

6. A
7. C
8. A
9. A
10. B

11. A
12. B
13. C
14. D
15. C

16. A
17. B
18. C
19. B
20. D

21. B
22. B
23. C
24. C
25. D

SOLUTIONS TO PROBLEMS

1. Actual cost = ($172)(.85)(.90) = $131.58 ≈ $132

2. Radius = .75', then area = (3.14)(.75)^2 ≈ 1.77 sq.ft.
   Since 1 sq.ft. = 144 sq.in., the area ≈ 254 sq.in.

3. 5'6" + 7'3" + 9'3 1/2" + 3'7 1/4" = 24'19 3/4" = 25'7 3/4"

4. Total area = (15)(21.25) + (18)(30.5) = 867.75 sq.ft.

5. .875 = 875/1000 = 7/8

6. 1 1/2 + 2 1/32 + 4 3/16 + 1 7/8 = 8 51/32 = 9 19/32 = 9.593

7. Third side = $\sqrt{9^2+12^2} = \sqrt{225} = 15"$

8. Let x = weight. Then, 12/32 = 5.75/x. Solving, x ≈ 15.33 lbs.

9. 12" = (3.14)(diameter), so diameter ≈ 3.82"

10. $\frac{39}{64}$" = .609375" ≈ .609"

11. Under his new contract, the weekly wage for 44 hours can be found by first determining his hourly rate for the first 40 hours = $431.40 ÷ 40 ≈ $10.80. Now, his time and one-half pay will = ($10.80)(1.5) = $16.20. His weekly wage for the new contract = $431.40 + (4)($16.20) = $496.20. His new hourly rate for 44 hours = $496.20 ÷ 44 ≈ $10.34. Under the old contract, his hourly rate for 44 hours was $415.20 ÷ 44 = $9.44. His hourly rate increase = $10.34 - $9.44 = $0.90. (Answer key: between $0.80 and $1.00)

12. 4'3 1/4" + 7'2 1/2" + 11' 1/4" = 22'6"

13. .038 = 38 thousandths

14. ($10.86)(40) + ($16.29)(3) = $483.27

15. 3'2 1/4" + 8 7/8" + 2'6 3/8" + 2'9 3/4" + 1'0" = 8'25 18/8" = 10'3 1/4"

16. The gear ratio is inversely proportional to the gear size. Let x = large gear's rpm. Then, 6/1 = 120/x. Solving, x = 20

17. Subtract 14 from 29.76

18. 5/8 = .625

19. Let x = number of pounds. Then, 300/450 = 100/x. Solving, x = 150

20. 600 quarts = 150 gallons, since 4 quarts = 1 gallon

21. (9")(9")(10") = 810 cu.in. Then, 810 ÷ 231 ≈ 3.5

22. Let x = unknown cost. Then, 30/$76.80 = 45/x. Solving, x = $115.20

23. $18,000 + ($18,000)(1.10) = $37,800

24. ($10.00)(1.15) = $11.50

25. 7/8" + 3/4" + 1/2" + 3/8" = 20/8" = 2 1/2"

TEST 2

DIRECTIONS: Each question or incomplete statement is followed by several suggested answers or completions. Select the one that BEST answers the question or completes the statement. *PRINT THE LETTER OF THE CORRECT ANSWER IN THE SPACE AT THE RIGHT.*

1. A sheet metal plate has been cut in the form of a right triangle with sides of 5, 12, and 13 inches.
   The area of this plate, in square inches, is

   A. 30   B. 32 1/2   C. 60   D. 78

   1.____

2. If steel weighs 480 lbs. per cubic foot, the weight of an 18" x 18" x 2" steel base plate is _____ lbs.

   A. 180   B. 216   C. 427   D. 648

   2.____

3. By trial, it is found that by using 2 cubic feet of sand, a 5 cubic foot batch of concrete is produced.
   Using the same proportions, the amount of sand, in cubic feet, required to produce 2 cubic yards of concrete is MOST NEARLY

   A. 7   B. 22   C. 27   D. 45

   3.____

4. The total number of cubic yards of earth to be removed to make a trench 3'9" wide, 25'0" long, and 4'3" deep is MOST NEARLY

   A. 53.1   B. 35.4   C. 26.6   D. 14.8

   4.____

5. A large number of 2 x 4 studs, some 10'5" long and some 6'5 1/2" long, are required for a job.
   To minimize waste, it would be PREFERABLE to order lengths of _____ feet.

   A. 16   B. 17   C. 18   D. 19

   5.____

6. A 6" pipe is connected to a 4" pipe through a reducer. If 100 cubic feet of water is flowing through the 6" pipe per minute, the flow, in cubic feet, per minute through the 4" pipe is

   A. 225   B. 100   C. 66.6   D. 44.4

   6.____

7. If steel weighs 0.28 pounds per cubic inch, then the weight, in pounds, of a 2" square steel bar 120" long is MOST NEARLY

   A. 115   B. 125   C. 135   D. 155

   7.____

8. A three-inch diameter steel bar two feet long weighs MOST NEARLY (assume steel weighs 480 lbs./cu.ft.) _____ lbs.

   A. 48   B. 58   C. 68   D. 78

   8.____

9. The area of a circular plate will be reduced by 5% if a sector removed from it has an angle of _____ degrees.

   A. 18   B. 24   C. 32   D. 60

   9.____

10. If a 4 1/16 inch shaft wears six thousandths of an inch, the NEW diameter will be _____ inches.

    A. 4.0031   B. 4.0565   C. 4.0578   D. 4.0605

11. A set of mechanical plan drawings is drawn to a scale of 1/8" = 1 foot.
    If a length of pipe measures 15 7/16" on the drawing, the ACTUAL length of the pipe is _____ feet.

    A. 121.5   B. 122.5   C. 123.5   D. 124.5

12. An electrical drawing is drawn to a scale of 1/4" = 1'. If a length of conduit on the drawing measures 7 3/8", the actual length of the conduit, in feet, is

    A. 7.5   B. 15.5   C. 22.5   D. 29.5

13. Assume that you have assigned 6 mechanics to do a job that must be finished in 4 days. At the end of 3 days, your men have completed only two-thirds of the job. In order to complete the job on time and because the job is such that it cannot be speeded up, you should assign a MINIMUM of _____ extra men.

    A. 3   B. 4   C. 5   D. 6

14. Assume that a trench is 42" wide, 5' deep, and 100' long. If the unit price of excavating the trench is $105 per cubic yard, the cost of excavating the trench is MOST NEARLY

    A. $6,805   B. $15,330   C. $21,000   D. $63,000

15. If the scale on a shop drawing is 1/4 inch to the foot, then the length of a part which measures 2 3/8 inches long on the drawing is ACTUALLY _____ feet.

    A. 9 1/2   B. 8 1/2   C. 7 1/4   D. 4 1/4

16. It is necessary to pour a new concrete floor for a shop. If the dimensions of the concrete slab for the floor are to be 27' x 18' x 6", then the number of cubic yards of concrete that must be poured is

    A. 9   B. 16   C. 54   D. 243

17. The jaws of a vise move 1/4" for each complete turn of the handle.
    The number of complete turns necessary to open the jaws 2 3/4" is

    A. 9   B. 10   C. 11   D. 12

18. Assume that a jobbing shop is to submit a price for a contract involving 300 pieces of work. Assume that material costs 50 cents per piece, labor costs $7.50 an hour, and a lathe operator can complete 5 pieces in an hour.
    If overhead is 40% of material and labor costs and the profit is 10% of all costs, the submitted price for the entire job will be

    A. $630.24   B. $872.80   C. $900.00   D. $924.00

19. The following formula is used in connection with the three-wire method of measuring pitch diameters of screw threads: $G=\dfrac{0.57735}{N}$, where G = wire size and N = number of threads per inch.
According to this formula, the proper size of wire for a 1"-8NC thread is MOST NEARLY

   A. .0722"   B. .7217"   C. .0072"   D. .0074"

20. A millimeter is 1/25.4 of an inch and there are 10 millimeters to a centimeter.
If a piece of stock measures 127 centimeters long, the length of the stock, in feet and inches, would be MOST NEARLY

   A. 2'1"   B. 4'2"   C. 8'4"   D. 41'8"

21. For a certain job, you will need 25 steel bars 1 inch in diameter and 4"6" long.
If these bars weigh 3 pounds per foot of length, then the TOTAL weight for all 25 bars is _____ pounds.

   A. 13.5   B. 75.0   C. 112.5   D. 337.5

22. If steel weighs 0.30 pounds per cubic inch, then the weight of a 2 inch square steel bar 90 inches long is _____ pounds.

   A. 27   B. 54   C. 108   D. 360

23. A concrete wall is 36' long, 9' high, and 1 1/2' thick. The number of cubic yards of concrete that were needed to make this wall is

   A. 14   B. 18   C. 27   D. 36

24. If the scale on a shop drawing is 1/2 inch to the foot, then the length of a part which measures 41/4 inches long on the drawing has a length of APPROXIMATELY _____ feet.

   A. 2 1/8   B. 4 1/4   C. 8 1/2   D. 10 3/4

25. If the allowable load on a wooden scaffold is 60 pounds per square foot and the scaffold surface area is 3 feet by 12 feet, then the MAXIMUM total distributed load that is permitted on the scaffold is _____ pounds.

   A. 720   B. 1,800   C. 2,160   D. 2,400

KEY (CORRECT ANSWERS)

1. A
2. A
3. B
4. D
5. B

6. B
7. C
8. A
9. A
10. B

11. C
12. D
13. A
14. A
15. A

16. A
17. C
18. D
19. A
20. B

21. D
22. C
23. B
24. C
25. C

5 (#2)

SOLUTIONS TO PROBLEMS

1. Area = (1/2)(base)(height) = (1/2)(5")(12") = 30 sq.in.

2. Volume = (18") (18") (2") = 648 cu.in. = 648/1720 cu.ft.
   Then, (480)(648/1720) = $\approx$ 180 lbs.

3. 2 cu.yds. = 54 cu.ft. Let x = required cubic feet of sand. Then, 2/5 = x/54. Solving, x = 21.6 (or about 22)

4. (3.75')(25')(4.25') = 398.4375 cu.ft. $\approx$ 14.8 cu.yds.

5. 10'5" + 6'5 1/2" = 16'10 1/2", so lengths of 17 feet are needed

6. The amount of water flowing through each pipe must be equal.

7. (2")(2")(120") = 480 cu. in. Then, (480)(.28) $\approx$ 135 lbs.

8. Volume = (π) (.125 ')^2 (2) $\approx$ .1 cu.ft. Then, (.1)(480) = 48 lbs.

9. (360°)(.05) - 18°

10. 4 1/16 - .006 = 4.0625 - .006 = 4.0565

11. 15 7/16" $\div$ 1/8" = 247/16 . 8/1 = 123.5. Then, (123.5)(1 ft.) = 123.5 ft.

12. 7 3/8" $\div$ 1/4" = 59/8 . 4/1 = 29.5   Then, (29.5)(1 ft.) = 29.5 ft.

13. (6)(4) = 24 man-days normally required. Since after 3 days only the equivalent of (2/3)(24) = 16 man-days of work has been 1 done, 8 man-days of work is still left. 16 $\div$ 3 = 5 1/3, which means the crew is equivalent to only 5 1/3 men. To do the 8 man-days of work, it will require at least 8 - 5 1/3 = 2 2/3 = 3 additional men.

14. (3.5')(5')(100') = 1750 cu.ft. $\approx$ 64.8 cu.yds. Then, (64.8)($105) $\approx$ $6805

15. 2 3/8" $\div$ 1/4" = 19/8 . 4/1 = 9 1/2 Then, (9 1/2)(1 ft.) = 9 1/2 feet

16. (27')(18')(1/2') = 243 cu.ft. = 9 cu.yds. (1 cu.yd. = 27 cu.ft.)

17. 2 3/4" $\div$ 1/4" = 11/4 . 4/1 = 11

18. Material cost = (300)($.50) = $150. Labor cost = ($7.50)(300/5) = $450. Overhead = (.40)($150+$450) = $240. Profit = .10($150+$450+$240) = $84. Submitted price = $150 + $450 + $240 + $84 = $924

19. 6 = .57735" $\div$ 8 = .0722"

20. 127 cm = 1270 mm = 1270/25.4" ≈ 50" = 4.2"

21. (25)(4.5') = 112.5' Then, (112.5X3) = 337.5 lbs.

22. (2")(2")(90") = 360 cu.in. Then, (360)(30) = 108 lbs.

23. (36')(9')(1 1/2') = 486 cu.ft. = 18 cu.yds. (1 cu.yd. = 27 cu.ft.)

24. 4 1/4" ÷ 1/2" = 17/4 . 2/1 = 8 1/2. Then, (8 1/2)(1 ft.) = 8 1/2 ft.

25. (12')(3') = 36 sq.ft. Then, (36)(60) = 2160 lbs.

TEST 3

DIRECTIONS: Each question or incomplete statement is followed by several suggested answers or completions. Select the one that BEST answers the question or completes the statement. *PRINT THE LETTER OF THE CORRECT ANSWER IN THE SPACE AT THE RIGHT.*

1. A right triangular metal sheet for a roofing job has sides of 36 inches and 4 feet. The length of the remaining side is

    A. 7 feet
    B. 6 feet
    C. 60 inches
    D. 90 inches

    1._____

2. A U.S. Standard Gauge thickness is given as 0.15625. This thickness, in fractions of an inch, is MOST NEARLY _____ inches.

    A. 1/8   B. 4/32   C. 5/32   D. 3/64

    2._____

3. The weight per 100 of sheet metal fasteners is given as 2/3 pound. The APPROXIMATE number of fasteners in a 2-pound package is

    A. 166   B. 200   C. 300   D. 266

    3._____

4. The decimal equivalent of 27/32 is MOST NEARLY

    A. 0.813   B. 0.828   C. 0.844   D. 0.859

    4._____

5. If a scaled measurement of 1'3" on the drawing of a sheet metal layout represents an actual length of 10"0", then the drawing has been made to a scale of _____ inch to the foot.

    A. 3/4   B. 1 1/4   C. 1 1/2   D. 1 3/4

    5._____

6. Two and two-thirds tees can be made from one sheet of steel. If 24 tees must be made, then the number of sheets required is

    A. 6   B. 7   C. 8   D. 9

    6._____

7. A main duct 20 inches in diameter discharges into two branch ducts. The sum of the areas of the branches is to be equal to the area of the main duct. One branch is 12 inches in diameter.
   The diameter of the other branch is _____ inches.

    A. 16   B. 12   C. 10   D. 8

    7._____

8. If steel weighs 480 lbs. per cubic foot, the weight of 10 sheets, each 6 feet by 3 feet by 1/32 inch, is _____ lbs.

    A. 2,700   B. 1,237   C. 270   D. 225

    8._____

9. The area, in square inches, of a right triangle that has sides of 12 1/2, 10, and 7 1/2 inches is

    A. 18 1/4   B. 37 1/2   C. 75   D. 60

    9._____

84

10. In making a container to hold 1 gallon (231 cu.in.) and to be 6 inches in diameter at the top and 8 inches in diameter at the bottom, the height must be, in inches,

    A. 10.0 B. 8.2 C. 4.6 D. 6

11. A sheet metal worker is given a job to make a transition piece from a 8 1/2" diameter duct to an 11 1/4" diameter duct. If the length of the transition piece is 5 1/2" for each inch change in diameter, then the length of the transition piece is

    A. 14 7/8" B. 15" C. 15 1/8" D. 15 1/4"

12. A duct layout is drawn to a scale of 3/8" to a foot. If the length of a run shown on the drawing scales 7 1/2", then the ACTUAL length of the run is

    A. 19'6" B. 19'9" C. 20'0" D. 20'3"

13. An 18" x 24" duct is to be connected to a 24" x 24" duct by means of an eccentric transition piece (3 sides flush). If the taper is to be 1" in 4", then the length of the transition piece is

    A. 6" B. 12" C. 18" D. 24"

14. Twenty-seven pairs of 3/8" diameter rods each 3'3 1/2" long are needed to support a duct.
    If the available rods are ten feet long, then the MINIMUM number of rods that will be needed to make the twenty-seven sets is

    A. 9 B. 12 C. 15 D. 18

15. A rectangular sheet metal air duct with open ends is 12 feet long and 15" x 20" in cross-section. If one square foot of the sheet metal weighs 1/2 pound, then the TOTAL weight of the duct is _____ lbs.

    A. 10 B. 17 1/2 C. 35 D. 150

16. The sum of 1/12 and 1/4 is

    A. 1/3 B. 5/12 C. 7/12 D. 3/8

17. The product of 12 and 2 1/3 is

    A. 27 B. 28 C. 29 D. 30

18. If 4 1/2 is subtracted from 7 1/5, the remainder is

    A. 3 7/10 B. 2 7/10 C. 3 3/10 D. 2 3/10

19. The number of cubic yards in 47 cubic feet is MOST NEARLY

    A. 1.70 B. 1.74 C. 1.78 D. 1.82

20. A wall 8'0" high by 12'6" long has a window opening 4'0" high by 3'6" wide. The net area of the wall (allowing for the window opening) is, in square feet,

    A. 86 B. 87 C. 88 D. 89

21. A worker's hourly rate is $11.36. 21.____
    If he works 11 1/2 hours, he should receive

    A. $129.84   B. $130.64   C. $131.48   D. $132.24

22. The number of cubic feet in 3 cubic yards is 22.____

    A. 81   B. 82   C. 83   D. 84

23. At an annual rate of $.40 per $100, what is the fire insurance premium for one year on a 23.____
    house that is insured for $80,000?

    A. $120   B. $160   C. $240   D. $320

24. A meter equals approximately 1.09 yards. 24.____
    How much longer, in yards, is a 100-meter dash than a 100-yard dash?

    A. 6   B. 8   C. 9   D. 12

25. A train leaves New York City at 8:10 A.M. and arrives in Buffalo at 4:45 P.M. on the same 25.____
    day. How long, in hours and minutes, does it take the train to make the trip?
    _____ hours, _____ minutes.

    A. 6; 22   B. 7; 16   C. 7; 28   D. 8; 35

KEY (CORRECT ANSWERS)

1. C
2. C
3. C
4. C
5. C
6. D
7. A
8. D
9. B
10. D

11. C
12. C
13. D
14. D
15. C
16. A
17. B
18. B
19. B
20. A

21. B
22. A
23. D
24. C
25. D

SOLUTIONS TO PROBLEMS

1. Let x = remaining side. Converting to inches, $x^2 = 36^2 + 48^2$ So, $x^2 = 3600$. Solving, x = 60 inches.

2. $.15625 = \dfrac{15,625}{100,000} = \dfrac{5}{32}$

3. 2 ÷ 2/3 = 3. Then, (3)(100) = 300 fasteners

4. 27/32 = .84375 ≈ .844

5. 1'3" ÷ 10 = 15" ÷ 10 = 1 1/2"

6. 24 ÷ 2 2/3 = 24/1.3/8 = 9

7. Area of main duct = $(\pi)(10^2) = 100\pi$. One of the branches has an area of $(\pi)(6^2) = 36\pi$. Thus, the area of the 2nd branch = $100\pi - 36\pi = 64\pi$. The 2nd branch's radius must be 8" and its diameter must be 16".

8. Volume = (1/384')(6')(3') = .046875 cu.ft. Then, 10 sheets have a volume of .46875 cu.ft. Now, (.46875)(480) = 225 lbs.

9. Note that $(7\ 1/2)^2 + (10)^2 = (12\ 1/2)^2$, so that this is a right triangle. Area = (1/2)(10")(7 1/2") = 371/2 sq.in.

10. $231 = \dfrac{h}{3}[(\pi)(3)^2 + (\pi)(4)^2 + \sqrt{(9\pi)(16\pi)}]$, where h = required height. Then,

    $231 = \dfrac{h}{3}(9\pi + 16\pi + 12\pi)$. Simplifying, $231 = 37\pi h/3$.
    Solving, h ~ 5.96" or 6"

11. 11 1/4 - 8 1/2 = 2 3/4. Then, (2 3/4)(5 1/2) = 11/4 .11/2 = 15 1/8

12. 7 1/2" ÷ 3/8" = 15/2 .8/3 = 20 Then, (20)(1 ft.) = 20 feet

13. 24" - 18" = 6" Then, (6")(4) = 24"

14. 3'3 1/2" = 39.5". Now, (27)(2)(39.5") = 2133". 10 ft. = 120". Finally, 2133 ÷ 120 = 17.775, so 18 rods are needed.

15. Surface area = (2)(12')(1 1/4') + (2)(12')(1 2/3') = 70 sq.ft. Then, (70)(1/2 lb.) - 35 lbs.

16. 1/12 + 1/4 = 4/12 = 1/3

17. $(12)(2\ 1/3) = 12/1 \cdot 7/3 = 28$

18. $7\ 1/5 - 4\ 1/2 = 7\ 2/10 - 4\ 5/10 = 6\ 12/10 - 4\ 5/10 = 2\ 7/10$

19. 47 cu.ft. = 47/27 cu.yds. = 1.74 cu.yds.

20. (8')(12.5') - (4')(3.5') = 86 sq.ft.

21. ($11.36)(11.5) = $130.64

22. 1 cu.yd. = 27 cu.ft., so 3 cu.yds. = 81 cu.ft.

23. $80,000 ÷ $100 = 800. Then, (800)($.40) = $320

24. 100 meters = 109 yds. Then, 109 - 100 = 9 yds.

25. 4:45 P.M. - 8:10 AM. = 8 hrs. 35 min.

THE USE AND CARE OF TOOLS

CONTENTS

I. INTRODUCTION.
    1. Definitions
    2. Safety Precautions.

II. MEASURING TOOLS
    1. General
    2. Standards of Measurement
        a. Standards of Length
        b. Standards of Screw Threads
        c. Standards of Wire and Sheet Metal
        d. Standards of Weight
    3. Useful Measuring Tools
        a. Levels
        b. Plumb Bobs
        c. Scrivers
        d. Rules or Scales
        e. Precision Tapes
        f. Squares
        g. Calipers and Dividers h. Micrometers
        i. Surface, Depth, and Height Gages
        j. Plug, Ring, and Snap Gages and Gage Blocks
        k. Miscellaneous Measuring Gages

III. NONEDGED TOOLS
    1. General
    2. Useful Nonedged Tools
        a. Hammers and Mallets
        b. Screwdrivers
        c. Wrenches
        d. Pliers and Tongs
        e. Clamping Devices
        f. Jacks
        g. Bars and Mattock
        h. Soldering Irons
        i. Grinders and Sharpening Stones
        j. Benders and Pulters
        k. Torchers
        l. Blacksmith's Anvils and Iron Working Tools
        m. Breast Drill and Ratchet Bit Brace
        n. Sheet Metal Tools

IV. EDGED HANDTOOLS
    1. General
    2. Useful Edged Handtools
        a. Chisels
        b. Files
        c. Knives

d. Scrapers
e. Punches
f. Awls
g. Shears, Nippers, and Pincers h. Bolt, Cable, and Glass Cutters
i. Pipe and Tube Cutters, and Flaring Tools
j. Reamers
k. Taps and Dies
l. Thread Chasers
m. Screw and Tap Extractors

THE USE AND CARE OF TOOLS

I. INTRODUCTION

1. Definitions

   a. Handtools are defined as hand powered and hand operated tools that are designed to perform mechanical operations.
   b. Measuring tools are defined as tools that will measure work. Measuring tools can be classed as precision and non-precision tools.

2. Safety Precautions

   It is extremely important for all concerned to recognize the possibilities of injury when using handtools and measuring tools.
   The following safety precautions are included as a guide to prevent or minimize personal injury:

   a. Make certain all tool handles are securely attached before using them.
   b. Exercise extreme caution when handling edged tools.
   c. Do not use a tool for a purpose other than that for which it was intended.
   d. Do not handle tools carelessly carelessly piling tools in drawers, dropping tools on hard surfaces, etc., can damage tools. Damaged tools can cause mishaps.
   e. Keep your mind on your work so that you do not strike yourself or someone else with a hammer or sledge.
   f. Do not carry edged or pointed tools in your pocket.
   g. Always wear goggles when chipping metal and when grinding edges on tools.
   h. Hold driving tools correctly so that they will not slip off the work surface.
   i. Use the right tool for the job. The wrong tool may damage materials, injure workers, or both,
   j. Do not use punches with improper points or mushroomed heads,
   k. Do not use a tool that is oily or greasy. It may slip out of your hand, causing injury.
   l. When using jacks, make certain to use blocking or other supports when lifting a vehicle, in case of jack failure.
   m. Make sure work to be cut, sheared, chiseled, filed, etc., is steadied and secure, to prevent the tool from slipping.
   n. When using a knife, always cut away from your body, except in the case of a spoke shave or draw knife.
   o. Use torches and soldering irons with extreme care to prevent burns and explosions. The soldering iron must be so placed that the hot point cannot come in contact with flammable material or with the body.
   p. Familiarize yourself with the composition and hardness of the material to be worked.

II. MEASURING TOOLS
1. General

Measuring tools are designed for measuring work accurately. They include level indicating devices (levels), noncalibrated measuring tools (calipers, dividers, trammels) for transferring dimensions and/or layouts from one medium to another, calibrated measuring tools (rules, precision tapes, micrometers) designed to measure distances in accordance with one of several standards of measurement, gages (go and no-go gages, thread gages) which are machined to pre-determined shapes and/or sizes for measurement by comparison, and combination tools such as a combination square which is designed to perform two or more types of operation.

2. Standards of Measurement
   a. Standards of Length

   Two systems, the English and Metric, are commonly used in the design of measuring tools for linear measurements. The English system uses inches, feet, and yards, while the Metric system uses millimeters, centimeters, and meters. In relation to each other, 1 inch is equivalent to 25.4 millimeters, or 1 millimeter is equivalent to 0.039370 inch.

   b. Standards of Screw Threads

   There are several screw thread systems that are recognized as standards throughout the world. All threaded items for Ordnance use in the United States, Great Britain, and Canada are specified in the Unified System. The existing inch-measure screw-thread systems should be understood despite the existence of the Unified System.

(1) Inch-measure systems
(a) Whitworth

Introduced in England in 1941. The thread form is based on a 55 thread angle, and the crests and roots are rounded.

(b) American National

The American National screw-thread system was developed in 1933. This system is based on the 60 thread angle and the flat crests and roots and is included in the following series:
1. Coarse thread sizes of 1 to 12 and 1/4 to 4".
2. The fine thread series in sizes 0 to 12 and 1/4 to 1 1/2".
3. The extra-fine thread series in sizes 0 to 12 and 1/2 to 2".
4. The 8-pitch series in sizes from 1 to 6".
5. The 12-pitch series from 1/2 to 6".
6. The 16-pitch series from 3/4 to 4".

(c) Classes of fit

The American National screw-thread system calls for four regular classes of fit.

Class 1. - Loose fit, with no possibility for interference between screw and tapped hole.

2. - Medium or free fit, but permitting slight interference in the worst combination of maximum screw and maximum nut.
3. - Close tolerances on mating parts may require this fit, applied to the highest grade of interchangeable work.
4. - A fine snug fit, where a screwdriver or wrench may be necessary for assembly.

NOTE: An additional Class 5, or jaw fit, is recognized for studs.

(2) Unified system

Since the whitworth and American National thread forms do not assemble because of the difference in thread angle, the 60 thread angle was adapted in 1949; however, the British may still use rounded crests and roots and their products will assemble with those made in United States plants. In the Unified system, class signifies tolerance, or tolerance and allowance. It is determined by the selected combination of classes for mating external and internal threads. New classes of tolerance are listed below: 3 for screws, 1A, 2A, and 3A; and 3 for nuts, IB, 2B, and 3B.

(a) Classes 1A and 1B, loose fit

A fit giving quick and easy assembly, even when threads are bruised or dirty. Applications: Ordnance and special uses.

(b) Classes 2A and 2B, medium fit

This fit permits wrenching with minimum galling and seizure. This medium fit is suited for the majority of commercial fasteners and is interchangeable with the American National Class 2 fit.

(c) Classes 3A and 3B, close fit

No allowance is provided. Applications are those where close fit and accuracy of lead and thread angle are required.

c. Standards of Wire and Sheet Metal

Sheet metal, strip, wire, and tubing are produced with thickness diameters or wall thicknesses, according to several gaging systems, depending on the article and metal. This situation is the result of natural development and preferences of the industries that produce these products. No single standard for all manufacturers has been established, since practical considerations stand in the way of adoption. In the case of steel, large users are thoroughly familiar with the behavior of existing gages in tooling, especially dies, and do not intend that their shop personnel be burdened with learning how preferred thicknesses behave. Another important factor is the sum total of orders of warehouse stock manufactured with existing gages. You must keep abreast of any change in availability of metals in these common gaging systems, as opposed to simplified systems.

For example; in the brass industry, the American Standards Association (ASA) numbers are said to be preferred for simplicity of stocking, but actually most of the metal is still made to Brown and Sharpe (B&S) gage numbers.

(1) Sheet metal gaging systems

Several gaging systems are used for sheet and strip metal.

    (a)   Manufacturer's standard gaging system (Mfr's std)

This gaging system is currently used for carbon and alloy sheets. This system is based on steel weighing 41.82 psf, 1 inch thick. Gage thickness equivalents are based on 0.0014945 in. per oz. per sq. ft.; 0.023912 in. per lb. per sq. ft. (reciprocal of 41.82 lb. per sq. ft. per in. thick); 3.443329 in. per lb. per sq. in.

    (b) U.S. standard gaging system (U.S. std)

This gaging system is obsolete except for stainless steel sheets, cold-rolled steel strip (both carbon and alloy), stainless steel tubing, and nickel-alloy sheet and strip.

    (c) Birmingham wire gaging system (BWG)

This gaging system is also called the Stubs iron wire gaging system, and is used for hot-rolled steel carbon and alloy strip and steel tubing.

    (d) Brown and Sharpe, or American wire gaging system (B&S or AWG)

This gaging system is used for copper strip, brass and bronze sheet and strip, and aluminum and wire magnesium sheet.

(2)   Wire gaging systems

    (a) Steel wire gaging system (SWG) or washburn & Moen gaging system

This gaging system is used for steel wire, carbon steel mechanical spring wire, alloy-steel spring wire, stainless steel wire, and so forth. Carbon steel or music wire (wire used in the manufacture of musical instruments) is nominally specified to the sizes in the American Steel & Wire Company music wire sizes, although it is referred to by a number of other names found in steel catalogs.

    (b) Brown & Sharpe (B&S) or American wire gaging system (AWG)

This gaging system is used for copper, copper alloy, aluminum, magnesium, nickel alloy, and other nonferrous metal wires used commercially.

(3)   Rod gaging systems

The Brown & Sharpe gaging system is used for copper, brass, and aluminum rods. Steel rods are nominally listed in fractional sizes, but drill rod may be listed in stubs steel wire gage or the twist drill and steel wire gage. It is preferable to refer to twist drill sizes in inch equivalents instead of the Stubs or twist drill numbers.

d. Standards of Weight

Two standards of weight that are most commonly used are the Metric and English weight measures.

(1)   Metric standards

The principal unit of weight in the Metric system is the gram (gm). Multiples of grams are obtained by prefixing the Greek words deka (10), hekto (100), and kilo (1,000). Divisions are obtained by prefixing the Latin words deci (1/10), centi (1/100), and milli (1/1000). The gram is the weight of 1 cubic centimeter of puje distilled water at a temperature of 39.2° F.; the kilogram is the weight of 1 liter (one cubic decimeter) of pureQdistilled water at a temperature of 39.2° F.; the metric ton is the weight of 1 cubic meter of pyre distilled water at a temperature of 39.2° F.

(2) English standards

The principal unit of weight in the English system is the grain (gr). We are more familiar with the ounce (oz), which is equal to 437.5 grains.

3. Useful Measuring Tools
   a. Levels
      (1) Purpose
         Levels are tools designed to prove whether a plane or surface is true horizontal or true vertical. Some levels are calibrated so that they will indicate the angle inclination in relation to a horizontal or vertical surface in degrees, minutes, and seconds.
   b. Plumb Bobs
      (1) Purpose
         The common plumb bob is used to determine true verticality. It is used in carpentry when erecting vertical uprights and corner posts of framework. Surveyors use it for transferring and lining up points. Special plumb bobs are designed for use with steel tapes or line to measure tank contents (oil, water, etc.).
   c. Scribers
      (1) Purpose
         Scribers are used to mark and lay out a pattern of work, to be followed in subsequent machining operations. Scribers are made for scribing, scoring, or marking many different materials such as glass, steel, aluminium, copper, and so forth.
   d. Rules or Scales
      (1) Purpose
         All rules (scales) are used to measure linear dimensions. They are read by a comparison of the etched lines on the scale with an edge or surface. Most scale dimensions are read with the naked eye, although a magnifying glass can be used to read graduations on a scale smaller than 1/64 inch.
   e. Precision Tapes
      (1) Purpose
         Precision tapes are used for measuring circumferences and long distances where rules cannot be applied.
   f. Squares
      (1) Purpose
         The purpose of a square is to test work for squareness and trueness. It is also used as a guide when marking work for subsequent machining, sawing, planing, and chiseling operations.
   g. Calipers and Dividers

(1) Purpose

Dividers are used for measuring distances between two points, for transferring or comparing measurements directly from a rule, or for scribing an arc, radius, or circle. Calipers are used for measuring diameters and distances, or for comparing dimensions or sizes with standards such as a graduated rule,

h. Micrometers

(1) Purpose

Micrometers are used for measurements requiring precise accuracy. They are more reliable and more accurate than the calipers listed in the preceding section.

i. Surface, Depth, and Height Gages

(1) Purpose

(a) Surface Gage

A surface gage is a measuring tool generally used to transfer measurements to work by scribing a line, and to indicate the accuracy or parallelism of surfaces.

(b) Depth Gage

A depth gage is an instrument adapted to measuring the depth of holes, slots, counterborers, recesses, and the distance from a surface to some recessed part.

(c) Height Gage

A height gage is used in the layout of jigs and fixtures, and on a bench, where it is used to check the location of holes and surfaces. It accurately measures and marks off vertical distances from a plane surface.

(d) Surface Plate

A surface plate provides a true, smooth, plane surface. It is often used in conjunction with surface and height gages as a level base on which the gages and parts are placed to obtain accurate measurements,

j. Plug, Ring, and Snap Gages and Gage Blocks

(1) Purpose

Plug, ring, and snap gages, and precision gage blocks are used as standards to determine whether or not one or more dimensions of a manufactured part are within specified limits. Their measurements are included in the construction of each gage, and they are called fixed gages; however, some snap gages are adjustable. In the average shop, gages are used for a wide range of work, from rough machining to the finest tool and die making. The accuracy required of the same type gage will be different, depending on the application. The following classes of gages and their limits of accuracy are standard for all makes:

Class XX(Male gages only).
Precision lapped to laboratory tolerances. For master or setup standards.

Class X

Precision lapped to close tolerances for many types of masters and the highest quality working and inspection gages.

Class Y

Good lapped finish to slightly increased tolerances for inspection and working gages.

Class Z

Commercial finish (ground and polished, but not fully lapped) for a large percentage of working gages in which tolerances are fairly wide, and where production quantities are not so large.

Class ZZ(Ring gages only)

Ground only to meet the demand for an inexpensive gage, where quantities are small and tolerances liberal.

k. Miscellaneous Measuring Gages
   (1) Purpose
   (a) Thickness (Feeler) Gages

   These gages are fixed in leaf form, which permits the checking and measuring of small openings such as contact points, narrow slots, and so forth. They are widely used to check the flatness of parts in straightening and grinding operations and in squaring objects with a try square.

   (b) Wire and Drill Gages

   The wire gage is used for gaging metal wire, and a similar gage is also used to check the size of hot and cold rolled steel, sheet and plate iron, and music wire. Drill gages determine the size of a drill and indicate the correct size of drill to use for given tap size. Drill number and decimal size are also shown in this type gage.

   (c) Drill Rods or Blanks

   Drill rods or blanks are used on line inspection work to check the size of drilled holes in the same manner as with plug gages. They are also used for setup inspection to check the location of holes.

   (d) Thread Gages

   Among the many gages used in connection with the machining and inspection of threads are the center gage and the screw pitch gages.

   1. Center gage

   The center gage is used to set thread cutting tools. Four scales on the gage are used for determining the number of threads per inch.

   2. Screw pitch gage

   Screw pitch gages are used to determine the pitch of an unknown thread. The pitch of a screw thread is the distance between the center of one tooth to the center of the next tooth.

   (e) Small Hole Gage Set

   This set of 4 or more gages is used to check dimensions of small holes, slots, groves etc., from approximately 1/8 to 1/2" in diameter.

8

- (f) Telescoping Gages
  These gages are used for measuring the inside size of slots or holes up to 6" in width or diameter.
- (g) Thread Cutting Tool Gages
  These gages provide a standard for thread cutting tools. They have an enclosed angle of 29 and include a 29 setting tool. One gage furnishes the correct form for square threads and the other for Acme standard threads.
- (h) Fillet and Radius Gages
  These gages are used to check convex and concave radii in corners or against shoulders.
- (i) Drill Point Gage
  This gage is used to check the accuracy of drill cutting edges after grinding. It is also equipped with a 6" hook rule. This tool can be used as a drill point gage, hook rule, plain rule, and a slide caliper for taking outside measurements.
- (j) Marking Gages
  A marking gage is used to mark off guidelines parallel to an edge, end, or surface of a piece of wood. It has a sharp spur or pin that does the marking.
- (k) Tension Gage
  This type of gage is used to check contact point pressure and brush spring tension in 1 ounce graduations.
- (l) Saw Tooth Micrometer Gage
  This special gage checks the depth of saw teeth in thousandths of an inch from 0 to 0.075 inch.

III. NONEDGED TOOLS
1. General

This title encompasses a large group of general purpose hand-tools. These tools are termed nonedged hand-tools because they are not used for cutting purposes and do not have sharpened or cutting edges. They are designed to facilitate mechanical operations such as clamping, hammering, twisting, turning, etc. This group includes such tools as hammers, mallets, and screwdrivers; which are commonly referred to as driving tools. Other types of nonedged tools are wrenches, pliers, clamps, pullers, soldering irons, torches, and many others of similar nature. Several types of pliers have cutting edges (exceptions to the rule).

2. Useful Nonedged Tools
   a. Hammers and Mallets
      (1) Purpose
         Hammers and mallets are used to drive nails, spikes, drift pins, bolts, and wedges. They are also used to strike chisels, punches, and to shape metals. Sledge hammers are used to drive spikes and large nails, to break rock and concrete, and to drift heavy timbers.
   b. Screwdrivers
      (1) Purpose

Screwdrivers are used for driving or removing screws or bolts with slotted or special heads.

c. Wrenches
   (1) Purpose

   Wrenches are used to tighten or loosen nuts, bolts, screws, and pipe plugs. Special wrenches are made to grip round stock, such as pipe, studs, and rods. Spanner wrenches are used to turn cover plates, rings and couplings.

d. Pliers and Tongs
   (1) Purpose

   Pliers are used for gripping, cutting, bending, forming, or holding work, and for special jobs. Tongs look like long-handled pliers and are mainly used for holding or handling hot pieces of metal work to be forged or quenched, or hot pieces of glass.

e. Clamping Devices
   (1) Purpose

   Vises are used for holding work on the bench when it is being planed, sawed, drilled, shaped, sharpened, riveted, or when wood is being glued. Clamps are used for holding work that cannot be satisfactorily held in a vise because of its shape or size, or when a vise is not available. Clamps are generally used for light work.

f. Jacks
   (1) Purpose

   Jacks are used to raise or lower work and heavy loads short distances. Some jacks are used for pushing and pulling operations, or for spreading and clamping.

g. Bars and Mattock
   (1) Purpose

   Bars are heavy steel tools used to lift and move heavy objects and to pry where leverage is needed. They are also used to remove nails and spikes during wrecking operations. The mattock is used for digging in hard ground, cutting Toots irnderground, und to loosen clay formations in which there is little or no rock. The mattock may also be used for light prying when no bars are available,

h. Soldering Irons
   (1) Purpose

   Soldering is joining two pieces of metal by adhesion. The soldering iron is the source of heat by melting solder and heating the parts to be joined to the proper temperature.

i. Grinders and Sharpening Stones
   (1) Purpose

   Grinders are devices that are designed to mount abrasive wheels that will wear away other materials to varying degrees. Special grinders are designed to receive engine valves. Sharpening stones are used for whetting or final sharpening of sharp edged tools that have been ground to shape or to a fine point on a grinder,

j. Benders and Pullers
   (1) Purpose

Benders are designed to facilitate bending brass or copper pipe and tubing. Pullers are designed to facilitate pulling operations such as removing bearings, gears, wheels, pulleys, sheaves, bushings, cylinder sleeves, shafts, and other close-fitting parts.

    k.   Torches

        (1)   Purpose

Torches are used as sources of heat in soldering, sweating, tinning, burning, and other miscellaneous jobs where heat is required.

    l.   Blacksmith's Anvils and Iron Working Tools

        (1)   Purpose

Blacksmith's anvils are designed to provide a working surface when punching holes through metal and for supporting the metal when it is being forged and shaped. Iron working tools such as flatters, fullers, swages, hardies, and set hammers are used to form or shape forgings. Heading tools are used to shape bolts.

    m.   Breast Drill and Ratchet Bit Brace

        (1)   Purpose

The breast drill and ratchet bit brace are used to hold various kinds of bits and twist drills used in boring and reaming holes and to drive screws, nuts, and bolts.

    n.   Sheet Metal Tools

        (1)   Purpose

Sheet metal working tools consist of stakes, dolly blocks, calking tools, rivet sets, and dolly bars. Punches, shears, and hammers are also sheet metal working tools. However, they are covered in other sections of this text. Rivet sets and dolly bars are used to form heads on rivets after joining sections of sheet metal and steel work. Stakes are used to support sheet metal while the metal is being shaped. Calking tools are used to shape joints of sheet metal. Dolly blocks are used conjunction with bumping body hammers to straighten out damaged sheet metal.

IV.   EDGED HANDTOOLS

    1.   General

Edged handtools are designed with sharp edges for working on metal, wood, plastic, leather, cloth, glass, and other materials. They are used to remove portions from the work or to separate the work into sections by cutting, punching, scraping, chiseling, filing, and so forth.

    2.   Useful Edged Eandtools

        a.   Chisels

           (1) Purpose

Chisels are made to cut wood, metal hard putty, and other materials. Woodworker's chisels are used to pare off and cut wood. Cold chisels are used to chip and cut cold metal. Some blacksmith's chisels are used to cut hot metal. A special chisel that is available is used to cut hard putty so that glass may be removed from its frame channel.

        b.   Files

           (1) Purpose

Files are used for cutting, smoothing off, or removing small amounts of metal.

c. Knives

(1) Purpose

Most knives are used to cut, pare, notch, and trim wood, leather, rubber, and other materials. Some knives used by glaziers are called putty knives; these are used to apply and spread putty when installing glass.

d. Scrapers

(1) Purpose

Some scrapers are used for trueing metal, wood, and plastic surfaces which have previously been machined or filed. Other scrapers are made to remove paint, stencil markings, and other coatings from various surfaces.

e. Punches

(1) Purpose

Punches are used to punch holes in metal, leather, paper, and other materials; mark metal, drive pins or rivets; to free frozen pins from their holes; and aline holes in different sections of metal. Special punches are designed to install grommets and snap fasteners. Bench mounted punching machines are used to punch holes in metal one at a time, or up to 12 holes simultaneously.

f. Awls

(1) Purpose

A saddler's awl is used for forcing holes in cloth or leather to make sewing easier. A scratch awl is used for making a center point or a small hole and for scribing lines on wood and plastics.

g. Shears, Nippers, and Pincers

(1) Purpose

Shears are used for cutting sheet metal and steel of various thicknesses and shapes. Nippers are used to cut metal off flush with a surface, and likewise to cut wire, light metal bars, bolts, and nails. Pincers are used to pull out nails, bolts, and pins.

h. Bolt, Cable, and Glass Cutters

(1) Purpose

Cutters or clippers are used to cut bolts, rods, wire rope, cable, screws, rivets, nuts, bars, strips, and wire. Special cutters are made to cut glass.

i. Piper and Tube Cutters, and Flaring Tools

(1) Purpose

Pipe cutters are used to cut pipe made of steel, brass, copper, wrought iron, and lead. Tube cutters are used to cut tube made of iron, steel, brass, copper, and aluminum. The essential difference is that tubing has considerably thinner walls are compared to pipe. Flaring tools are used to make single or double flares in the ends of tubing,

j. Reamers

(1) Purpose

Reamers are used to smoothly enlarge drilled holes to an exact size and to finish the hole at the same time. Reamers are also used to remove burrs from the inside diameters of pipe and drilled holes,

k. Taps and Dies
   (1) Purpose

Taps and dies are used to cut threads in metal, plastics, or hard rubber. The taps are used for cutting internal threads, and the dies are used to cut external threads.

l. Thread Chasers
   (1) Purpose

Thread chasers are used to re-thread damaged external or internal threads,

m. Screw and Tap Extractors
   (1) Purpose

Screw extractors are used to remove broken screws without damaging the surrounding material or the threaded hole. Tap extractors are used to remove broken taps.

GLOSSARY OF METAL WORKING

CONTENTS

	Page
Abrasive ...... Base Metal	1
Bastard ...... Brass	2
Brass Bound ...... Cadmium	3
Calipers ...... Cobolt	4
Cold Chisel ...... Drift	5
Drill Bit ...... Fish Plate	6
Flaring ...... Gunmetal	7
Hacksaw ...... Hollowing Hammer	8
Iron ...... Malleable	9
Mallet ...... Ore	10
Oxidation or Oxidization ...... Post vise	11
Pumice ...... Rust	12
Safe Edge ...... Smooth cut	13
Snap head ...... Steel sheet	14
Stock ...... Tinner's or Tinman's Solder	15
Tinning ...... Wing nut	16
Wiped joint ...... Zinc Chloride	17
Properties of Metals	18
Properties of Alloys	18
Soldering Fluxes	19
Composition of Some Alloys	19

GLOSSARY OF METAL WORKING

A

ABRASIVE
A natural or artificial substance used for grinding, polishing, buffing, lapping or sandblasting. Commonly includes garnet, emery, corundum, diamond, aluminum oxide and silicon carbide.

ACID PICKLE
Diluted acid used for cleaning metal.

AGE HARDEN
The capacity of some metals to get harder as they get older.

ALLOY
A substance having metallic qualities, composed of one or more chemical elements, at least one of which is a metallic element.

ALUMINUM
Lightweight soft white-colored metal, usually alloyed with other metals to increase its hardness and other qualities.

ANGLE IRON
Mild steel. Bars with 90 degree cross-section.

ANNEALING
Treating metal to make it as soft as possible (usually by heating and cooling slowly). The necessary technique varies between metals and alloys.

ANODIZING
Chemical surface treatment for protection and decoration of aluminum and its alloys.

ANTIQUEING
Darkening copper or brass by chemical treatment.

ASBESTOS
Fibrous silicate mineral that is incombustible.

ASH
Springy hard wood used for hammer and mallet handles.

B

BALL PEIN
Hemispherical end of a hammer head.

BASE METAL
At one time, the name for common metals. They are contrast to the "noble" metals which are valuable.

BASTARD
A grade of fairly coarse file.

BEAK OR BICK
Round conical end of an anvil or stake. Also horn.

BELL MOUTH
Spread end of tube.

BICK IRON
Light anvil for sheet metalwork.

BIT
Jaws of tongs. A drill.

BLIND RIVETING
Using tubular rivets on a mandrel with a device for closing each rivet from one side of the metal.

BLOCKING HAMMER
A hammer with two large flat faces.

BLOWLAMP
A torch burning gas, kerosene or other fuel to produce a flame in the form of a jet.

BOLSTER
Block with hole to support work being punched.

BOLT
Screw fastening with a head to take a nut. Only threaded part of its length. If it is threaded fully to its head, it is a metal-threaded screw.

BORAX
Flux for hard soldering and brazing.

BOSS
Center part of a wheel. A locally raised part of sheet metal. The punch used to raise it.

BOSSING MALLET
Wooden mallet with an egg-shaped head for shaping sheet metal.

BOUGE
Knock out dents in raised work over a stake.

BRAKE
Mechanical device for folding sheet metal.

BRASS
An alloy consisting mainly of copper and zinc to which small amounts of other metals may be added. Common brass is yellow.

BRASS-BOUND
    Strengthened with brass straps. Particularly a wooden box or chest.

BRASS SCRIBER
    Pointed brass rod used to mark tinplate.

BRASS TONGS
    Tongs for dipping non-ferrous metals in acid pickles.

BRAZING
    Joining by melting spelter or hard solder.

BRAZING HEARTH
    Trough to hold coke or asbestos and support work while it is brazed.

BRONZE
    Copper alloy with tin and other metals.

BRONZE AGE
    Early period after the Stone Age when primitive man made tools and implements from an early form of copper alloy.

BUFF
    To polish the surface of metal with a powered buffing wheel.

BUFFING WHEEL
    Fabric disks held together, usually by sewing, forming a wheel to be rotated at high speed and used for polishing. Also called a polishing mop.

BURIN
    An engraving tool.

BURNISHER
    Hard steel rubbing tool. Shaping tool used in metal spinning.

BURR
    Turned over edge. Small rotary file.

BUTTERFLY NUT
    A nut to fit on a bolt with projections for hand tightening. Also a wing nut.

BUTT STRAP
    Riveted strip over meeting edges. Also a fish plate.

<u>C</u>

CADMIUM
    Metal used for plating steel to protect it from corrosion.

CALIPERS
Tool with hinged curved jaws for checking thickness and diameters.

CANISTER STAKE
Cylindrical stake with a flat end.

CARBIDE TIP
A very hard tip to make a cutting edge bonded to tool steel, using carbide, which is a compound of carbon with one or more metallic elements.

CARBON
Element added to iron to make steel.

CARRIAGE BOLT
Bolt with a shallow domed head and square neck to prevent it from turning in wood.

CARRIAGE SCREW
A large wood screw with a head to take to wrench.

CASTING
Melting metal and pouring it into molds.

CENTER PUNCH
Pointed punch to make a dot in metal.

CENTIGRADE or CELSIUS
Temperature scale with the freezing point of water 0 degrees and the boiling point 100 degrees.

CHALK LINE
Fine cord that is used with chalk to strike a line.

CHATTER MARKS
Ridges produced by vibration during filing or other work.

CHISEL
An end-cutting tool for wood or metal.

CHROMIUM
Metal that can be alloyed with steel or used for plating.

CHUCK
A holding device for a drill or a lathe. A former for metal spinning.

CIRCUMFERENCE
Distance around a circle or other rounded shape. A similar distance around an angular shape is a perimeter.

COBOLT
Rare metal which can be added to steel to increase its magnetic properties.

COLD CHISEL
A tool that is hammered for cutting cold metal.

CORROSION
Oxidization of the surface of metal such as rust on iron.

CORRUGATED IRON
Sheet iron or steel ridged and grooved regularly across its width. It is usually protected by galvanizing.

COPPER
Red colored non-ferrous metal.

COUNTERSINK
Bevelled edge of hole. The tool for doing this.

CREASING HAMMER
A hammer with two narrow cross peins.

CREASING IRON
Stake with grooves across.

CROCUS
Fine polishing powder.

CURVE ALLOWANCE
Size correction at a bend due to measuring around the neutral axis.

D

DEVELOPMENT
Outline of the shape while metal is flat that will give the desired shape after bending.

DIAMETER
Distance across a circle.

DIE
Tool for cutting a screw thread on a rod. A form into which metal is pressed for shaping.

DIVIDERS
Hinged pair of points for scratching a circle or comparing distances

DRAW FILLING
Using a file sideways along an edge to remove cross file marks.

DRAWING
Pulling metal through holes to form wire.

DRIFT
Punch used to draw holes into line.

DRILL BIT
Tool for making a hole by cutting (as distinct from punching).

DRILL PRESS
A machine which uses drill bits to make holes.

E

ELEMENT
Any of about 100 substances that cannot be revolved by chemical means into simpler substances.

EMBOSS
Raise sheet metal, with a hammer, punch or boss from the reverse side.

EMERY
Grit used as abrasive on metal.

ESCUTCHEON
Key hole or the plate around it.

ETCHING
Eating into metal with acid to produce a design, usually a name.

EXCRUDING
Forcing metal through a die to form rods of special section.

EYE BOLT
Bolt with flattened or shaped end with a hole through.

F

FAHRENHEIT
Common temperature scale.

FERROUS
Alloy containing iron.

FERRULE
A tube or cap on a wooden handle to prevent it from splitting.

FILE
Tool with teeth made with grooves cut across it.

FILE CARD
Wire brush for cleaning files.

FISH PLATE
Alternative name for butt strap.

FLARING
    Spreading the end of a tube. Giving it a bell mouth.

FLANGE
    Folded edge.

FLASH
    The movement of solder as it melts around a joint. Excess solder to be removed.

FLUX
    Liquid or powder used to help a metal or an alloy to flow in welding, brazing or soldering.

FOCUS
    Plural is foci. Point about which a curved shape is generated, The center of a circle is its focus. An ellipse has two foci.

FOLDING BARS
    Parallel bars used for bending sheet metal.

G

GALVANIZED IRON
    Iron coated with zinc as a protection against rust.

GAUGE
    Size, particularly the thickness of sheets or the diameter of wires, according to a recognized scale. The tool for measuring this.

GILDING
    Coating with gold leaf.

GILDING METAL
    Alloy of copper and zinc with a greater proportion of copper than in brass.

GOLD
    One of the rare or noble metals.

GRAVER
    Cutting tool with a diamond-shaped cutting point.

GROOVING STAKE
    Alternative name for a creasing iron.

GUILLOTINE
    Large mechanical shearing machine.

GUNMETAL
    Alloy of copper and tin.

H

HACKSAW
Metal-cutting handsaw with its blade tensioned in a frame.

HALF-MOON STAKE
A hatchet stake with a curved edge.

HARD SOLDER
Copper/zinc alloy with other metals added to lower its melting point.

HATCHET SOLDERING IRON
An iron with a copper bit at an angle to the shaft and a straight thin edge.

HATCHET STAKE
Stake with straight sharp edge for bending sheet metal across its top.

HEARTH
Any container for coke or other solid fuel.

HEAT TREATMENT
Heating steel to alter its character. This includes annealing, hardening, tempering and normalizing. Annealing other metals by heating.

HEEL
Opposite end of anvil or bick iron to the beak.

HICKORY
Springy wood used for mallet and hammer handles.

HIDE MALLET
A mallet with a head formed from rolled leather.

HIGH CARBON STEEL
Steel with sufficient carbon to permit hardening and tempering.

HOLD UP
Support one rivet head while the other is formed.

HOLLOW GROUND
A concave bevel on a cutting edge.

HONING
Sharpening or smoothing with a fine abrasive stone.

HORN
Alternative name for beak of anvil or bick iron.

HOLLOWING HAMMER
A hammer with two ball peins.

I

IRON
Silver-white common metal which can be alloyed with carbon to make steel.

IRON AGE
A prehistoric age when man first learned how to make tools and weapons from iron.

J

JAWS
Gripping surfaces of tongs or vise.

JENNY
Hand-operated machine for flanging and wiring sheet metal edges.

K

KILLED SPIRITS
Zinc chloride used as flux when soldering.

L

LEAD
Heavy and soft grey metal. The amount a nut moves forward in one revolution on a threaded rod.

LEG VISE
A strong vise attached to a bench, but with a leg extending to the floor.

LOW CARBON STEEL
Steel that does not contain the proper amount of carbon to permit tempering. Also called mild steel.

M

MACHINIST'S VISE
Vise with a parallel action to mount on a bench.

MAGNESIUM
Very light and combustible metal.

MALACCA
Species of cane used for mallot handles.

MALL OR MAUL
Large two-handed mallet.

MALLEABLE
Capable of being shaped.

MALLET
Type of hammer with wood, rawhide or plastic head.

MANDREL OR MANDRIL
Iron block on which parts are shaped. Particularly a round cone for shaping rings.

MEAN
Average or center. A mean line is the center of the thickness of bent sheet metal.

MILD STEEL
Low-carbon steel which cannot be tempered.

METALLURGY
The science and technology of metals.

MICROMETER
Instrument for making fine measurements using the rotation of a screw.

MUSHROOM STAKE
A round-topped steel anvil.

N

NEUTRAL AXIS
The mean line in the thickness of metal that is neither stretched nor compressed when it is bent.

NIBBLER
Shearing tool that removes particles along a line.

NICKEL
Metal alloyed with steel and used for plating.

NOBLE METALS
At one time the name for valuable metals in contrast with the "base" metals.

NON-FERROUS
Alloy that does not contain iron.

NORMALIZE
Reduce internal stresses after working by heating and allowing to cool slowly in the same way as annealing steel.

O

OFFSET
Double bend to alter alignment of a bar or sheet.

ORE
Solid naturally occurring mineral aggregate from which metal is extracted.

OXIDATION OR OXIDIZATION
   The effect of air on the surface of metal.

P

PATINA
   Colored oxidation on metal surfaces due to long exposure to air particularly on bronze. It can be simulated by chemical action.

PEEN, PEIN or PANE
   The shaped end of a hammer head.

PEENING
   Hollowing with ball peen hammer.

PERIMETER
   Distance around an angular outline. A similar measurement around a curve is a circumference.

PICKLE
   Dilute acid for cleaning metals.

PIERCING
   Cutting internal fretted shapes in sheet metal with a fine saw in a frame.

PITCH
   Composition for supporting repousse work. Distance between holes or the tops of a screw thread.

PLANISHING
   Hammering all over to harden and decorate.

PLANISHING HAMMER
   A hammer with highly polished flat or domed faces.

PLATE
   Alternative name for sheet metal. Usually of the thickert types.

PLATINUM
   Rare and valuable metal used especially in jewelry.

PLIERS
   Small gripping tool with tongs action.

POP RIVETING
   Alternative name for blind riveting.

POST VISE
   Alternative name for a leg vise.

PUMICE
: Volcanic powder used as a fine abrasive.

PUNCH
: Tool intended to be hit with a hammer to make a dent or hole.

Q

QUENCH
: To cool hot metal quickly in a liquid.

R

RADIUS
: Distance from the center to the circumference of a circle.

RAISING
: Making a deep bowl shape by hammering over a stake.

RAISING HAMMER
: A hammer with two cross peins.

RASP
: A coarse file type of tool with teeth individually raised.

RAKE
: Cutting angle of a drill or other tool.

REPOUSSÉ
: Method of raising a pattern from the back of thin metal.

REPOUSSÉ HAMMER
: Light hammer with broad-faced pein.

ROLLING
: Squeezing metal between rollers to form sheets.

ROUGE
: Fine polishing powder.

ROUT
: Cut grooves or hollows.

RULE
: Measuring tool. Not "ruler."

RUST
: Corrosion on iron steel.

S

SAFE EDGE
One edge of a file without teeth. Turned-in edge of sheet metal.

SAND BAG
Leather bag containing sand on which hollowing is done.

SATE
Alternative name for a sett. Used to flatten metal.

SCALLOP
An evenly waved edge.

SCREW
A fastening to take a nut that threaded to the head. If it is only threaded part way, it is a bolt. A screw can cut its own thread in wood or sheet metal.

SCOTS SHEARS
Large snips.

SCRIBE OR SCRIBER
Hard sharp steel point for scratching metal.

SECOND CUT
The grade of file commonly used on edges of sheet metal.

SELF-TAPPING SCREW
Hardened steel screw that cuts its thread in sheet metal.

SET
A hammer-like head on a wooden handle that is hit with a hammer to shape metal.

SET SCREW
Screw used to draw parts together.

SHANK
The neck or part of a tool between the handle and the blade.

SHEAR
Large snips that are often bench mounted with a lever handle.

SILVER SOLDER
Copper/zinc alloy with a small amount of silver included to lower its melting point.

SLEDGE
A large two-handed hammer.

SMOOTH CUT
The finest grade file normally used.

SNAP HEAD
Raised round head on a rivet.

SNIPS
Scissor action shears for cutting sheet metal.

SOFT SOLDER
Low melting point solder. A lead/tin alloy.

SOLDER
Alloy used to fuse into joints. The action of soldering.

SOLDERING IRON
Tool with copper bit that is heated to melt solder.

SPATULA
Iron rod with flattened end that is used to place flux and spelter in brazing or for hard soldering.

SPELTER
Form of brass used in brazing.

SPINNING
Shaping sheet metal in a lathe.

SPRING STEEL
High carbon steel that is similar to tool steel.

SQUARE
As a setting out term, this means at right angles.

STAINLESS STEEL
Steel alloyed with other metals to resist corrosion.

STAKE
Shaped block used as an anvil in sheet metalwork.

STAKE VISE
Alternative name for leg vise.

STEEL
Alloy of iron and carbon.

STEEL PLATE
Steel rolled into sheets more than about three-sixteenths of an inch thick.

STEEL SHEET
Steel rolled thinner than steel plate.

STOCK
Supply of metal. The body of a tool. One head of a lathe.

STRIKE A LINE
Draw a line using a chalked cord.

STROP
Leather strap used in the final stages of tool sharpening.

SULFURIC ACID
Corrosive fluid used in cleaning metal.

SWAGE BLOCK
Large block with many hollows and holes.

SWARF
Filings and other waste removed from metal.

T

TAIL
Oppposite end of anvil or bick iron to the beak. Also heel.

TANG
Part of a tool that is driven into a handle.

TAP
Tool for cutting a screw thread in a hole.

TEMPER
Reduced full hardened steel to a lesser hardness and less brittle form for a particular use.

TEMPLATE or TEMPLET
Pattern used for marking around to transfer an outline.

THREE-SQUARE FILE
A file with a triangular cross section.

TIN
White metal used in alloys and for coating steel for protection against corrosion.

TINMAN'S or TINNER'S MALLET
Mallet with a cylindrical wood head.

TINNER
Worker in tinplate.

TINNER'S or TINMAN'S SOLDER
Lead/tin alloy. Also called soft solder.

TINNING
   In soldering, coating the bit or the surfaces to be joined with soft solder,

TINPLATE
   Thin sheet steel that is coated with tin.

TINSNIPS
   Small shears for cutting sheet metal.

TINSMITH
   Alternative name for tinner or tinman.

TORCH
   Device for burning gas to produce a forced flame that can be adjusted to size.

TRACER
   Narrow-ended punch used for decorative lines.

TRAMMEL HEADS
   Sliding heads on a bar for use as large compasses or dividers.

TRIPOLI
   A fine polishing compound.

TRUNCATED
   Cut off. Usually applied to part of a cone.

V

VISE
   Two-jawed device with a tightening screw. Attached to bench and used to hold metal being worked on.

VISE GRIP PLIERS
   Pliers that can be locked on to the work.

VISE CLAMPS
   Sheet metal covers that are placed over vise jaws.

W

WELD
   Fuse two pieces of metal together with heat.

WHITING
   Powder used for polishing tinplate.

WING NUT
   Alternative name for butterfly nut.

WIPED JOINT
    Joint between pipes made with plumber's solder.

WIRE EDGE
    Burr on the edge of a sharpened tool.

WIRED EDGE
    Wire enclosed in a rolled sheet metal edge.

WORK HARDEN
    Hardening due to hammering or other work on non-ferrous metals.

WRENCH
    Any tool for levering or twisting. Particularly useful for turning nuts and bolts.

WROUGHT IRON
    Iron with little or no carbon. Produced by the puddling process

<u>Z</u>

ZINC
    Grey/white metal used mainly in alloys and for coating steel

ZINC CHLORIDE
    Chemical used as a flux for soldering.

Properties of Metals

Metal	Chemical symbol	Pounds per cubic in.	Melting Point Degrees F
Aluminum	Al	0.0924	1218
Cadmium	Cd	0.3105	610
Chromium	Cr	0.2347	2939
Cobolt	Co	0.3123	2696
Copper	Cu	0.3184	1981
Gold	Au	0.6975	1945
Iron (wrought)	Fe	0.2834	2750
Lead	Pb	0.4105	621
Magnesium	Mg	0.0628	1204
Nickel	Ni	0.3177	2646
Silver	Ag	0.3802	1761
Tin	Sn	0.2632	449
Zinc	Zn	0.2587	787

Properties of Alloys

Alloy	Composition	Pounds Per Cubic Inch	Melting Point Degrees F
Brass Or	80 copper, 20 zinc	0.3105	1846
Spelter	60 copper, 40 zinc	0.3018	1634
	50 copper, 50 zinc	0.2960	1616
Solder	20 tin, 80 lead	-	532
	40 tin, 60 lead	-	446
	40 tin, 60 lead	-	446
	50 tin, 50 lead	-	401
	60 tin, 40 lead	-	369
	70 tin, 30 lead	-	365
	90 tin, 10 lead	-	419
Steel	-	0.2816	2500

Soldering Fluxes

Prepared fluxes can be purchased, but the following are traditional fluxes for soft soldering. For hand soldering all suitable metals, use borax.

Metal Or Alloy	Flux
Aluminum	Stearin
Brass	Chloride of zinc or resin
Copper	
Lead	Chloride of zinc or resin
Tinned steel	
	Tallow or resin
	Chloride of zinc or resin
Galvanized steel	Hydrochloric acid
Zinc	Hydrochloric acid
Pewter	Gallipoli oil
Iron and steel	Chloride of zinc or chloride of ammonia

Composition of Some Alloys

Alloy	copper	lead	tin	zinc	Antimony
Brass	32	-	1.5	10	-
Gunmetal	80	-	10	-	-
Gilding metal	60	-	-	40	-
Bell metal	80	-	20	-	-
Spelter	50	-	-	50	-
Solder	-	60	40	-	-
Britannia metal	2	-	90	-	8
Pewter	2	2	89	-	7
Type metal		50	25	0	25

www.ingramcontent.com/pod-product-compliance
Lightning Source LLC
Chambersburg PA
CBHW082209300426
44117CB00016B/2732